DISCOVER

AF177739

wish
e in
Cologne

Visualisation of the planned mural in St Mary's Chapel in Cologne Cathedral (→ p. 19)

✡ *DISCOVER*COLOGNE

PUBLISHER'S INFORMATION

A city walk
Discover – Jewish life in Cologne
By John Sykes

© 2025 All rights reserved
BKB Verlag GmbH
Auerstraße 4
50733 Köln
www.bkb-verlag.de

Cover design & Layout:
Petra Nyenhuis, BRANDTMedia
Printing: Brandt GmbH, Bonn

ISBN 978-3-96722-065-0

BKB Verlag GmbH
Auerstraße 4
50733 Köln
Telefon 0221 9521460
www.bkb-verlag.de
mail@bkb-verlag.de

Cologne has a rich Jewish heritage
that goes back more than 1,700
years. It is the only city in Germany
with written evidence of Jewish
settlement in Roman times. Traces of
Jewish history in the Middle Ages and
modern times can be found all over
the city in buildings, museums and
memorial places – and in the stories of
Jewish residents who contributed to
the economic and cultural life of the
city, including the composer Jacques
Offenbach, the banker and major con-
tributor to Cologne Cathedral Abraham
Oppenheim, and three leaders of the
movement to establish a Jewish state
in Palestine. This is not only a story of

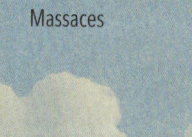

pogroms and Holocaust, but also of periods of prosperity, thriving cultural activities and peaceful coexistence with Christian neighbours.

This book provides in compact form a guide to this history and to the living Jewish community that exists today in Cologne, a city that is proud to be twinned with and to maintain fruitful contacts with Tel Aviv. We take a walk through the historic city centre, where the great cathedral and the city hall tell of the relations between Jews and Christians, and to the site of the medieval Jewish quarter, where a new museum and archaeological zone are arising. We find stories of Jewish life in the shopping district and in the New Town, where a fine synagogue stands today. Jewish cemeteries and places of memorial in the outer districts of Cologne are included, as well as an outline of the Jewish community in the present day.

This guide presents a lively, varied and moving history, an account of good times and bad times. Enjoy your exploration of Jewish Cologne!

COLOGNE CATHEDRAL

Inside and outside the cathedral are many depictions of Jews – from the Middle Ages and modern times, on stained-glass windows, painted, carved in wood and stone, and also on the golden shrine of the Three Magi. A stone inscription from the archbishop dated 1266 confirms rights of the Jewish community.

MA'ALOT

The open space named Heinrich-Böll-Platz and the Ma'alot sculpture were designed by the Israeli artist Dani Karavan. His work relates to its surroundings – the cathedral, Rhine, rail tracks – to Jewish religious practices and to Christian pilgrimages.

MIQUA

Archaeological work in the medieval Jewish quarter next to city hall has yielded exciting results. Remains of the synagogue and ritual bath, as well as a great variety of items found in the excavations, will be displayed in the Archaeological Quarter and MiQua museum, currently under construction.

BOCKLEMÜND CEMETERY

An extensive area of the Westfriedhof in the western suburb of Bocklemünd became the main Jewish cemetery in Cologne in 1918, and is still in use today. Trees and lawns surround graves and monuments, including some remains that were transferred from the medieval burial ground.

YAVNE MEMORIAL CENTRE AND LION FOUNTAIN

In front of the Memorial Centre, with its exhibition on the schools and members of the Orthodox community that once stood here, a proud Lion of Juda roars on a fountain commemorating the Jewish children of Cologne who were murdered in the Holocaust.

SYNAGOGUE

The synagogue in Roonstrasse on Rathenauplatz is an imposing domed building, inaugurated in 1899, devastated in 1938 and reopened in 1959. It is now the principal centre of Jewish life in Cologne, and receives visitors for events and guided tours.

NS-DOK

The multi-media exhibition dedicated to the victims of Nazi persecution movingly documents the fate of the Jewish population of Cologne in the years 1933 to 1945.

1. The Roman Harbour Road
2. Ma'alot
3. The Cathedral
4. St. Andreas Church
5. Haus Goldschmidt
6. Alter Markt and City Hall
7. The Historic Jewish Quarter
8. Galeria/Schildergasse
9. Antoniterkirche
10. Dischhaus
11. Stadtmuseum
12. Offenbachplatz
13. Glockengasse
14. Law Courts
15. NS-DOK

Café Reichard
Manufactum

Köln Hbf

Unter Sachsenhausen
An den Dominikanern
Dominikanerkirche St. Andreas (4)
Komödienstraße
Trankgasse
Café Reichard
(3) Kölner Dom
MA'ALOT
(5)
Heinrich-Böll-Platz
(2)
Museum Ludwig
Bischofsgartenstr.
Roncalliplatz
(15)
Appellhofplatz
(1) Römische Hafenstraße
Am Hof
(14)
Neven-DuMont-Str.
Breite Str.
Auf d. Ruhr
Turmstraße
Minoritenstr.
(11)
Ludwigstraße
Unter Goldschmied
Burgestr.
Rathaus-platz
(6)
Glockengasse
(13)
(12)
Kolumbastr.
Brückenstr.
(10) Dischhaus
Manufactum
Marspfortengasse
Obenmarspforten
Alter Markt
(7)
Offenbachplatz
Herzogstraße
Marsplatz
Antoniterkirche (9)
Schildergasse
(8)
Hohe Straße
Große Sandkaul
Gürzenichstraße
Deutzer Brücke
Cäcilienstraße
Cäcilienstraße
Pipinstraße
Heumarkt

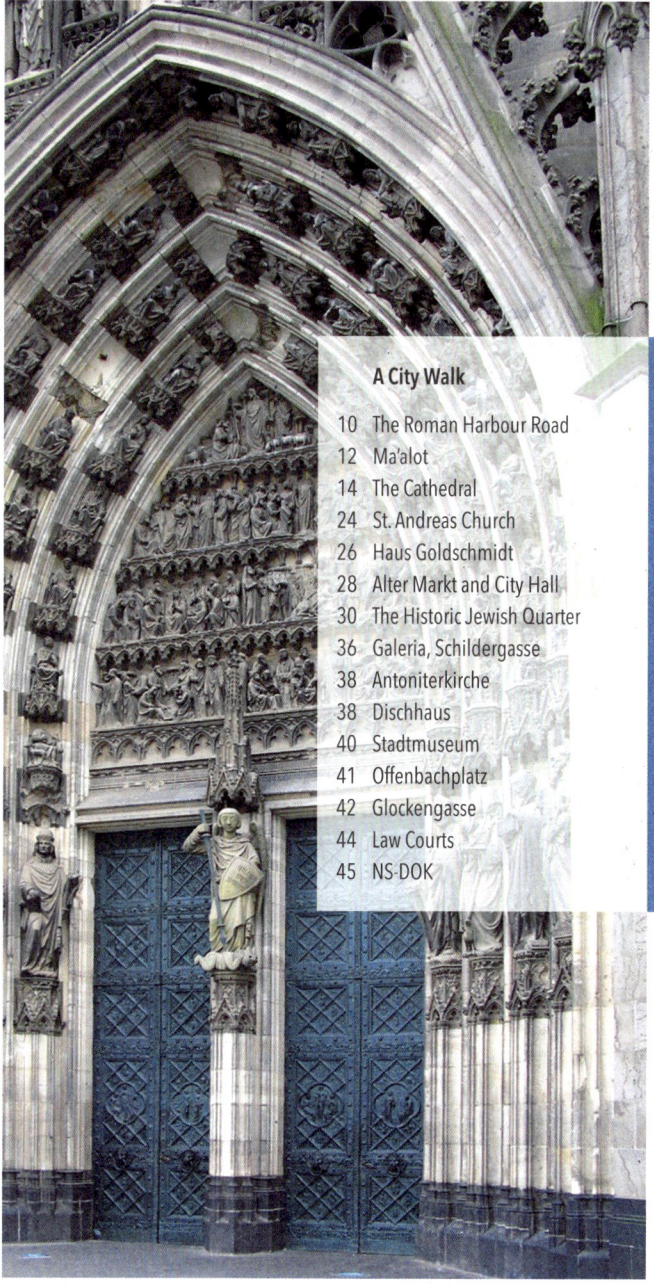

A CITY WALK

On this walk through the city centre, we begin in Roman times, learn about Jewish-Christian relations in and around the cathedral, and look at Jewish life in the Middle Ages and the 19th century around the city hall. Then we pass through shopping streets where Jewish families ran businesses until the 1930s, visit the site of a synagogue devastated in 1938, and finish at an exhibition devoted to the victims of Nazi persecution.

THE ROMAN HARBOUR ROAD ①

On the east side of Roncalliplatz next to the Roman-Germanic Museum, steps lead down to the remains of a Roman road. The basalt stones, re-laid here in the 1970s, were part of a road connecting to the Roman quayside. The first Jews who arrived in Roman Cologne probably came by boat on the Rhine, and may have used this road to enter the city.

Cologne is the only city in Germany for which written evidence exists of Jewish settlement in Roman times. A letter dated 321 CE from the court of Emperor Constantine to the curia (city council) of Cologne states that Jews may become council members. Historians interpret this to mean that a prosperous Jewish community existed at that time, because only the wealthy could be admitted to the curia: if there was a shortfall in tax collection, its members had to make up the difference.

There is no archaeological evidence in Cologne – and very little in other parts of Germany – for a Jewish population in Roman times. The Roman-Jewish wars and the destruction of the temple in Jerusalem in 70 CE were an important cause of the diaspora, the scattering of Jewish people across the ancient world. The late 1st century was a period of growth in Roman Cologne, when trade on the Rhine expanded and the city wall with its gates and roads was built. Perhaps Jewish merchants came to the Rhineland at this early date – but the letter written in the 4th century is all the evidence that we have.

● At the lower end of the Roman road, walk up the steps immediately to your left and go straight ahead. Just before you reach the cathedral, turn right. Next to the entrance to the Museum Ludwig, set into the red tiles of the paving, you will see a long path of grey granite with an iron rail in the middle. Follow it until you reach a sculpture in the shape of a small, stepped tower on the east side of the square called Heinrich-Böll-Platz.

MA'ALOT ②

The granite path, the tower sculpture and the design of the entire Heinrich-Böll-Platz form an installation entitled Ma'alot, made in 1986 by the Israeli artist Dani Karavan. Ma'alot is a biblical Hebrew word derived from a word meaning "ascend". It denotes psalms no. 120–134, the "songs of ascension" sung in Jerusalem when priests carried jugs of water up to the temple. From the river bank, steps lead up to the Ma'alot tower. This is the route once taken by Christian pilgrims ascending to the cathedral.

Ma'alot relates to its surroundings: the metal rail to the station and railway bridge, the granite to the paving around the cathedral, the red tiles to the architecture of the Museum Ludwig. Karavan's environment also includes six acacia and nine sycamore trees. According to the book of Exodus the ark of the covenant was made from acacia wood, and the sycamores are intended as a reference to one type of timber used in King Solomon's temple.

The numbers six and nine recur in Karavan's design: the tower sculpture has six steps, and the stone platform on the south side of the square, placed directly above the conductor's podium in the concert hall below, consists of six concentric circles. Genesis tells us that God created the world in six days; six million Jews died in the Holocaust, and the slits in the sculpture at the end of the iron rail reveal a view across the Rhine to the Deutz district, from where Cologne Jews were taken by train to the death camps. However, Karavan rejected any explicit interpretation of his work, saying only that "I touch memory." The choice of an artist from Tel Aviv is one example of many in Cologne of the efforts made in Germany for reconciliation with the Jewish people.

In 2011, for the 25th anniversary of Karavan's installation, 300 singers from Tel Aviv and Cologne sang the Ma'alot psalms that pilgrims sang on the steps of the temple in Jerusalem. In the Philharmonie concert hall, which lies beneath Heinrich-Böll-Platz, young musicians from Tel Aviv joined a youth orchestra from Cologne to celebrate the 200th anniversary of the composer Jacques Offenbach (→ p. 28), who was born into a Cologne Jewish family, and the 40th anniversary of the partnership between the two cities.

🌐 www.maalot.de (in German)

EAST END OF THE CATHEDRAL ③

There are many depictions of Jews in Cologne Cathedral and various associations of the cathedral with the Jewish community. Depictions of scenes from Jewish scriptures, for Christians the Old Testament, show Jews without anti-Semitic content. Other depictions are clearly anti-Jewish.

➲ Walk from Heinrich-Böll-Platz to the east end of the cathedral and stand by the wall of the priests' cemetery. You will see a stone crucifix below the central window. On the buttress immediately to the right, just higher than the top of the window, is a water spout in the shape of a pig. This is an example of the notorious "Judensau", the *"Jew-sow"* Ⓐ, showing a Jew suckling the teats of a pig. This insulting motif appears in more than 40 places in German-speaking regions, usually on churches. Here the pig is plainly visible, held in place by a metal frame, but the small human figure under its belly is more difficult to see.

MICHAELSPORTAL ⑧

On the north side of the cathedral, facing the station, are three entrances. The restoration of the sculptures on the middle one, the *Michaelsportal*, (→ p. 9) dating from 1879–81, was revealed in 2024 after years of work. The Bible scenes above the door are flanked by four rows of arches with 57 saints, the patrons of different professions, who are seated beneath stone canopies. On the left, in the second row from the centre, one figure is missing. This was **Werner of Oberwesel**, patron of wine makers. He worked for a Jewish family, and when he was found dead in Bacharach on the Rhine in 1287, aged 16, a rumour spread that he was murdered by Jews who drank the blood of young Christians in their rituals. Pogroms along the rivers Rhine and Moselle followed and a chapel dedicated to Werner, now ruined, was built in Bacharach. Not until 1963 did the Roman-Catholic diocese of Trier abolish the cult of St Werner. When the Michaelsportal was restored, the decision was taken not to renew the figure of Werner, which showed him in anti-Semitic tradition holding a martyr's palm.

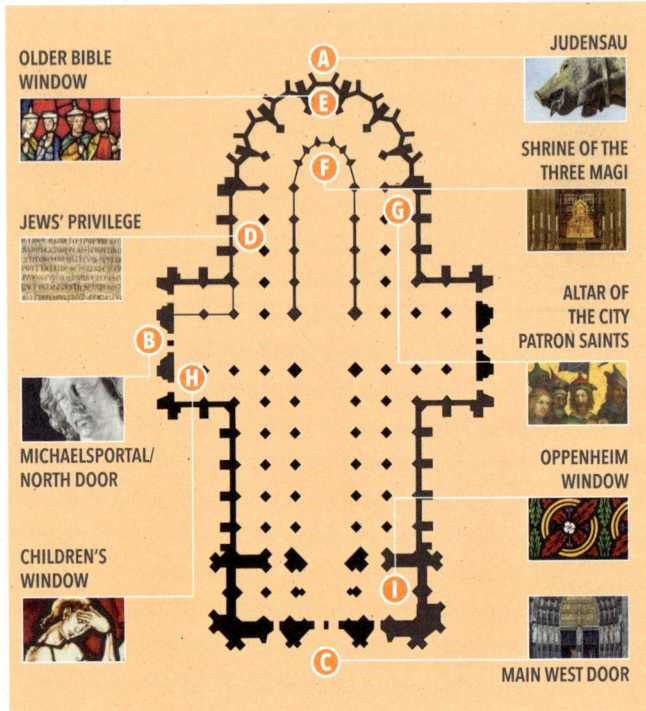

OLDER BIBLE WINDOW

JUDENSAU

JEWS' PRIVILEGE

SHRINE OF THE THREE MAGI

ALTAR OF THE CITY PATRON SAINTS

MICHAELSPORTAL/ NORTH DOOR

OPPENHEIM WINDOW

CHILDREN'S WINDOW

MAIN WEST DOOR

INSIDE THE CATHEDRAL

MAIN DOOR ©

As you enter the cathedral through the *main door in the west*, you pass sculptures of figures from the Jewish scriptures: on the left Adam, Noah with the ark, Moses with the tablets, King David with a harp, the prophet Elijah; on the right Eve, Abraham holding a knife for sacrifice, Samuel with a horn, Solomon with a model of the temple. The roots of Christianity in Jewish history and religion are, of course, depicted in many places inside and outside the cathedral.

JEWS' PRIVILEGE ⓓ

➡ Once inside, walk along the north aisle to the Chapel of the Cross. A tall stone tablet on the north wall bears a Latin inscription. This is the so-called *Jews' Privilege*. Dated 1266, this is a

public confirmation of rights that the archbishop gave to the Jewish community, which was under his protection. It states that the Jews could bury their dead without disturbance in their cemetery south of the city wall, that they would not pay higher customs duties than Christians, and that they had a monopoly of money-lending in the city. In return for allowing Jews to live and trade in Cologne, the archbishops taxed them, and also borrowed money from the Jews at times. This tablet made from French limestone, over two metres tall with finely carved lettering, shows the importance of the Jewish community to the archbishops in the Middle Ages.

OLDER BIBLE WINDOW Ⓔ

The middle window in the central chapel at the east end of the cathedral dates from the year 1260 and is known as the *Older Bible Window*. It illustrates the Christian belief that events of the Jewish scriptures, the Old Testament, prefigured the New Testament, that the life of Jesus fulfilled the older prophecies. Here we see scenes from the Old Testament on the left, and matching events from the New Testament next to them on the right. The seventh row from the bottom depicts the Weaning of Isaac. Abraham gave a feast to celebrate this event. We see people sitting at a table, the men wearing pointed hats. On the right, a servant takes Isaac away from his mother's breast. The pointed hats identify the figures as Jews – not a sign of discrimination, but simply the traditional headgear seen in medieval depictions of Jews. The New Testament scene alongside is the Last Supper.

SHRINE OF THE THREE MAGI Ⓕ

➡ Now turn around and look at the golden Shrine of the Three Magi in its glass case. The scene on the lower left is the Flagellation of Christ. The two men who are whipping Jesus wear the pointed hats of Jews and have hate-filled facial expressions. This is a clearly anti-Semitic representation, depicting Jews as evil persons. By contrast the Bible tells us that Pontius Pilate ordered the whipping, i.e. it would have been done by Roman soldiers, not Jews.

ALTAR OF THE CITY PATRON SAINTS Ⓖ

On the east wall of the Lady Chapel (Chapel of St Mary) on the south side of the cathedral is the *Altar of the City Patron Saints*. It was painted in 1442 by Stefan Lochner and shows the Three Magi presenting their gifts on the centre panel. The other patron saints of Cologne are St Ursula with her followers, on the left, and the Roman soldier St Gereon with a Christian legion, on the right. This altar once stood on the east wall of the city hall chapel, a building that had been the synagogue until the expulsion of Jews from Cologne in 1424. It occupied the exact spot where the ark holding the torah scrolls had stood. To make a clear statement against the anti-Jewish depictions in the cathedral, in 2026 a new work of art will be painted on the wall above the altar: on a black background, the stone foundation which supported both the ark in the synagogue and the altar painting, will be shown in its original size. This work by Andrea Büttner (→ p. 1) represents the interlinked Jewish and Christian history of Cologne, and connects the cathedral to the site of the medieval Jewish quarter (→ p. 22).

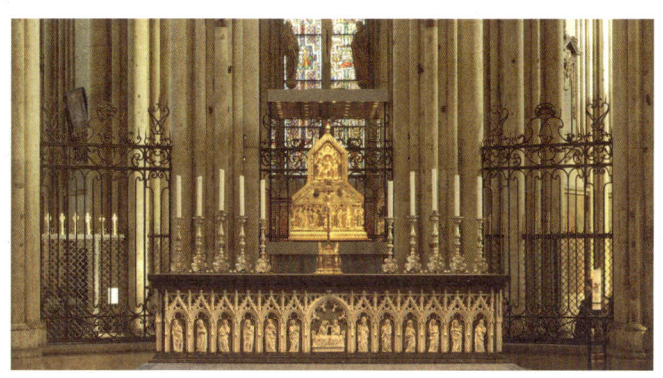

von Oppenheim

CHILDREN'S WINDOW Ⓗ

➡ From here, we go to the *Children's Window*, on the right when you face the west wall of the north transept. The window was financed by children's donations and installed in 1965. On each horizontal row are four scenes with a shared theme: on the left from Jewish scriptures, two in the middle from the New Testament, on the right a modern scene involving children. The theme of the sixth row from the bottom is betrayal: on the left, Joseph is sold into slavery by his brothers, in the middle Judas accepts 30 pieces of silver from the priest (whose face echoes insulting portrayals of Jews by the Nazis) and grabs the arm of Jesus. On the right a mother and her children flee from bombing in the Second World War, above them aircraft and the smoke of explosions. To put this last scene in the context of betrayal is a shocking example of the survival of anti-Semitism into the post-war years: the Nazis claimed that the war resulted from a Jewish conspiracy to betray the German people.

OPPENHEIM WINDOW ①

We conclude on a note of reconciliation in the space beneath the *south tower*. The window on the right on the south wall was donated in the 1880s by the Oppenheim family, Jewish bankers who played a leading role in the regional economy. At the bottom of the window we see, between coats of arms, achievements of which the Oppenheims were proud: on the right are depictions of a factory, a Rhine steamship and a railway, on the left four buildings that they financed: the synagogue, the glass palace of the Flora gardens, a children's hospital – and Cologne Cathedral.

The Oppenheims and other Jews made major contributions to the cathedral in the 19th century, when its completion was regarded as both a national project and a work of civic pride in Cologne, not merely a task for Roman-Catholic Christians. The synagogue shown on the window was designed by Ernst Friedrich Zwirner, the cathedral architect. There was Jewish-Christian cooperation in the Middle Ages, too, when stone carvers from the cathedral workshop made the ornamental surround of the bimah, where the Torah was read in the synagogue. Today, at www.koelner-dom.de/en/tour/cologne-cathedral-and-the-jews) and in a special tour, Cologne Cathedral gives frank, self-critical explanations of anti-Semitic representations that can be seen there, including a second "Judensau" in the choir stalls that can only be viewed as part of the guided tour

🌐 www.koelner-dom.de/en/tour/cologne-cathedral-and-the-jews)

INFORMATION

📍 Domkloster 4
🕐 6am–8pm
🌐 www.koelner-dom.de

Have a
break

Opposite the cathedral is one of Cologne's finest traditional cafés: the **Café Reichard** with excellent cakes, light meals at lunchtime, and outdoor seating with a view of the cathedral towers.

📍 Unter Fettenhennen 11
🕐 daily 8.30am–7pm
🌐 www.cafe-reichard.de

Tombstone of Rachel, Stadtmuseum Köln

THE JEWISH COMMUNITY IN THE MIDDLE AGES

The story of Jewish Cologne is not only about discrimination and pogroms. There were periods of prosperity and cultural flowering. In the Middle Ages many Jewish communities flourished along the river Rhine, where Mainz, Worms and Speyer were further important centres of Jewish culture. Through finance, a business not generally open to Christians because the Church prohibited usury, and trade, Jews acquired wealth and ran a self-governing community at the

heart of Cologne, the largest and wealthiest city in Germany at that time. In legal disputes between Christians and Jews, jurisdiction was in the hands of the Jewish court of law. Men of learning from Cologne such as Ascher ben-Jehiel, a rabbi and expert on Talmudic law who was born in the Rhineland in the 1250s and died in Toledo in 1327, enjoyed Europe-wide prestige in Jewish circles.

The wealth of Jews and the privileges given to them by the archbishop attracted hostility. They were also victims of the rivalry between the citizens and the archbishops, who ruled the city until it gained de facto independence in 1288. The rich merchants who dominated the city council disliked disorder, but did not act effectively to prevent the pogrom of 1349 and were quick to take possession of Jewish property afterwards. As the city authorities did not benefit from the tax levied on Jews by the archbishop, in 1424 they refused to renew the permission granted every ten years for Jews to live in Cologne. One reason given to justify this was that the holy Christian city of Cologne should be free from non-believers, but in truth the Jewish community fell victim to greed and a power struggle.

ST. ANDREAS CHURCH ④

This church, dedicated to St Andrew, is 200 metres ahead and slightly to the right when you stand with your back to the cathedral towers. In the cathedral we have seen items that show how Christianity represented Jews both in a hostile way and as precursors of Christianity.

A further striking example of this ambiguity stands in the south transept of St. Andreas. A *shrine* made from gilded copper holds holy relics revered by Christians, supposedly the skulls and bones of the seven *Maccabean brothers*, said to have been brought to Cologne in 1164 at the same time as the relics of the Three Magi.

In the second century BCE, Antiochus IV, ruler of the Seleucid Empire, tried to prohibit Jewish religious practices. According to the second Book of Maccabees (not considered a canonical part of the Hebrew or Protestant Christian Bible), he ordered seven Jewish brothers to eat pork in his presence. When they refused, they were cruelly tortured and killed before the eyes of their mother. The lower part of the shrine depicts the martyrdom of the brothers; above and parallel to this are events from the passion and crucifixion of Christ,

whose mother Mary also witnessed her son's death. In this way, Jews who died for their faith were venerated as martyrs, and the Church appropriated Jewish victims of persecution.

LÜPERTZ WINDOWS

Most of the *stained-glass windows* in this church are modern works *by Markus Lüpertz*. Those around the shrine, installed in 2008, tell the story of the Maccabean martyrs in bold colours. In the central window, Mary and the infant Jesus can be seen at the top with symbols of the Holy Trinity – an eye, a hand, a dove. Below are the skulls of the Maccabee brothers, one of them with a yellow Star of David, the emblem that Jews were forced to wear under Nazi rule, as an eye. The window on the right shows the deposition of Jesus from the cross, and below this the heads of Maccabees boiled in a cauldron of oil. On the left, below the crucifixion, the bloody severed limbs of the brothers seem to bloom like roses. The shrine and windows express the idea that salvation and new life arise from martyrdom and suffering, and represent the Christian interpretation of Jewish history and scripture as prefiguring the events of the New Testament. By contrast, for Jews the Maccabean revolt against Antiochus symbolises strength and resistance. The name "Maccabees" is given to Jewish sports clubs, for example the well-known football club Maccabi Tel Aviv. The sports section of Cologne's Jewish community is called Makkabi Köln.

INFORMATION

⊙ Andreaskloster 1
⊘ Mon–Fri 7.30am–6pm,
Sat 8.30am–6.30pm, Sun 8.30am–7pm,
no visits during church services
⊕ dominikaner-koeln.de
www.romanische-kirchen-koeln.de

HAUS GOLDSCHMIDT ⑤

➡ From the church, walk back towards the cathedral and turn right to the start of the Hohe Strasse. The building on the right after you pass a small alley is Haus Goldschmidt. It has two round windows at first-floor level with stone sculptures and was once the residence and jeweller's shop of the Jewish Goldschmidt family, who opened their first store in this street in 1878. In 1928 they built Haus Goldschmidt in its prestigious location opposite the cathedral with the address Domkloster No. 1.

In the 19th and early 20th century, many Jewish families ran businesses in the city centre, often selling clothing. By 1939 at the latest, all were forced to close down or sell, usually at a price much below the true value. Ernst Goldschmidt, the last owner, his mother Caroline and his brother Hans Rudolf fled to the Netherlands, were deported from there and killed in the death camp of Sobibor in 1943. Look down to see three square metal plaques in the paving. They are called Stolpersteine, "stumbling stones", and record the fate of this family.

➡ Walk a few steps south along Hohe Strasse, turn left into Am Hof, and follow this road past the fountain on your right and down.

STUMBLING STONES – STOLPERSTEINE

"A person is only forgotten when his or her name is forgotten". This saying from the Talmud is the idea of the Stolpersteine, brass plaques over which passers-by stumble – not physically, but visually and in their thoughts – on streets in German cities and some other European countries. In 1992 the artist Günther Demnig began to lay them in front of houses that were once occupied by Jewish families. In May 2023, Demnig laid his 100,000th Stolperstein. The names, dates of birth and death, and fates – deportation to death camps, emigration, suicide – are engraved on the plaques. They can be seen in many places in the centre and suburbs of Cologne. At Obenmarspforten no. 13, on the way from the MiQua to the Galeria department store, look out for plaques for four members of the Hannes family: "Theo Hannes lived here, born 1903, fled to France, interned in Drancy, deported 1942, murdered in Auschwitz." All are marked on an interactive map on a dedicated app for smartphones, with texts in English and German.

🌐 www.stolpersteine.eu

HIER WOHNTE
CAROLINE
GOLDSCHMIDT
GEB. MARCUS
JG. 1866
FLUCHT 1939 HOLLAND
INTERNIERT WESTERBORK
DEPORTIERT 1943
SOBIBOR
ERMORDET 9.7.1943

HIER WOHNTE
HANS RUDOLF
GOLDSCHMIDT
JG. 1899
FLUCHT 1938 HOLLAND
INTERNIERT WESTERBORK
DEPORTIERT 1943
SOBIBOR
ERMORDET 9.7.1943

HIER WOHNTE
ERNST RICHARD
GOLDSCHMIDT
JG. 1894
FLUCHT 1937 HOLLAND
INTERNIERT VUGHT
WESTERBORK
DEPORTIERT 1943
SOBIBOR
ERMORDET 7.5.1943

HIER WO
UND ARB
JOHANNA
GEB. L

D WOHNTE
STE

ALTER MARKT AND CITY HALL ⑥

In the middle of the marketplace you have a good view of the city hall tower. It was completed in 1414, badly damaged in the Second World War and renewed in the post-war years. 124 figures in niches on five levels, installed in the 1990s, represent persons of significance in the history of Cologne. Eight of them honour people from Jewish families.

CITY HALL TOWER

The man with a tall hat at the left corner on the middle level is the composer *Jacques Offenbach*. He was born Jakob Offenbach in 1819. His father was the cantor (musician) of the synagogue in Cologne. Young Jakob was a virtuoso cellist who wrote his own compositions and played dance music in taverns in a trio. At the age of 14 he went to Paris to study at the Conservatoire and took the French name Jacques, but often returned to visit the city of his birth.

At his right elbow, round the corner on the south façade, is a non-religious man of Jewish origin: *Karl Marx*, who edited the Rheinische Zeitung newspaper in Cologne in 1842-43, and its successor the Neue Rheinische Zeitung in 1848-49. Marx came from a family of rabbis on both his mother's and father's side, but his father converted to Christianity.

The figure next-but-one to the right of Offenbach is *Moses Hess* (1812–75, → p. 65), a utopian socialist who is depicted with a young man holding a banner with the words "liberty, equality, fraternity". Hess collaborated with Marx as a journalist and was an influential early advocate of Zionism, the movement to establish a Jewish state in Palestine. He died in Paris but was buried at his own wish in the Jewish cemetery in Cologne-Deutz. In 1962 his mortal remains were taken to Israel and reburied at the Sea of Galilee.

To the right of Hess, the man holding a conductor's baton is **Ferdinand Hiller** (1811–85), director of music in the city of Cologne for 30 years. The second figure from the right in this row is **Abraham Oppenheim** (→ p. 43). One level higher, the third figure from the left is **Hertha Kraus** (1897–1968, → p. 77), head of the social services in Cologne from 1923 until 1933, when she emigrated to the USA.

Two further persons of Jewish origin are on the north side of the tower: **Edith Stein** (top level, 2nd from right, → p. 47) and **Max Isidor Bodenheimer** (4th level on the right, → p. 51).

City hall tower, 1st figured from left: Abraham Oppenheim

THE HISTORIC JEWISH QUARTER ⑦

➡ From Alter Markt walk up the steps next to the city hall tower and go left. Behind the Gothic windows to the south of the city hall loggia lies the 14th-century *Hansasaal*. In this hall the twinning agreement between Cologne and Tel Aviv was signed in 1979. On the wall at its south end are statues of nine historic heroes, among them Judas Maccabaeus, the leader of a Jewish revolt against Antiochus IV, a ruler who wanted to suppress the Jewish religion.

MIQUA

A new museum and archaeological trail devoted to Roman and Jewish history, the *MiQua*, is under construction in front of the city hall (planned opening: 2027). This site was the Jewish quarter from the 11th century until 1424, and also the Christian goldsmiths' quarter.

INFORMATION

🕐 Public guided tours in English: Sun 10:30am

In 1135 about 30 houses in the quarter were owned by Jews, with some 300 residents. 200 years later, about 800 people, 2% of the city population, occupied 75 houses. For the 12th and 13th centuries, the records show evidence of good neighbourly relations between Jews and Christians, and there was no strict separation of their properties – in one case, a latrine and the costs of cleaning it were shared between a Jewish and a Christian-owned house. From the late 13th century, relations deteriorated. Outward-facing doors and windows of Jewish homes were closed off, and at night the gates of the quarter were locked – but strictly speaking it was not a ghetto, as the Jewish community held the keys.

Community buildings also stood here: the synagogue and the mikveh (ritual bath), a bakehouse for bread and for keeping meals warm on the Shabbat, a hostel for travellers and a hall for celebrations and meetings. Remains of these facilities were found during archaeological work in the 1950s. At the same time, foundations and walls of the Roman governor's palace, the praetorium, were uncovered.

City Hall Square with the future MiQua (right p. 31) and the Renaissance loggia on the left (p. 30). Image: HHVISION

Renewed excavations after 2007 prepared the opening of the **MiQua** ("**M**useum **i**n the **Qu**arter"), which will present an archaeological trail with remains of the synagogue and praetorium and an exhibition including items found on this site.

SYNAGOGUE

A *synagogue* was built in the early 11th century and restored after the pogrom of 1096 (→ p. 84). Alterations made in the 13th century suggest that the Jewish community was flourishing. The bimah – the platform where the Torah scrolls were read – was adorned with a Gothic screen of fine French limestone, made by stone carvers from the cathedral workshops. It was smashed during the pogrom of 1349, but its appearance has been reconstructed from 3,000 fragments. After the expulsion of Jews from the city in 1424, the synagogue was converted into a chapel for the city hall and fulfilled this purpose until 1795. Later it was used as a storehouse, the home of a male-voice choir, then as a church for Old Catholics and, in the 1930s, Anglicans. Bombing in World War II destroyed it.

MIKVEH

The *mikveh* was built next to the synagogue in the 12th century. The subterranean changing room, above which there was probably a tower, adjoins a shaft with a depth of 17 metres. Steps lead to a stone basin at the bottom in which groundwater collected. Ritual cleansing involved total immersion of the naked body in this naturally collected water – manual filling of the basin was not allowed. The ritual was prescribed for women after menstruation and childbirth, and performed by men on some occasions, for example if they had touched a corpse. After 1424 the mikveh was filled in, used as a latrine and forgotten until it was rediscovered in the 1950s.

ARCHAEOLOGICAL TRAIL

When the long-awaited opening of the MiQua takes place, the city of Cologne will possess a unique attraction. It will combine an archaeological trail below street level with an exhibition on the upper levels showing a major collection of items, many of which were found on this very site, illuminating both the medieval Jewish quarter and the story of Jews and Judaism after their expulsion from Cologne in 1424 and up to the present day. A number of museums about Jewish history exist in Germany, and historic Jewish sites can be seen in other European countries, but nowhere else is it possible to see such an exhibition directly above the buildings where Jews lived for centuries. At the same time, the MiQua will present the impressive remains of the praetorium and other Roman remains, over which the Jewish quarter was built. During construction work, the route from Alter Markt to Unter Goldschmied via steps next to the city hall tower is blocked at times. In this case, from the south end of Alter Markt turn right to Marsplatz and Obenmarspforten.

INFORMATION

⊙ Obenmarspforten/Unter Goldschmied
⊕ miqua.lvr.de

Cologne excavation find from the Jewish quarter

DIGGING UP HISTORY

In excavations on the site of the MiQua, the archaeologists found many remarkable artefacts. They include a chess piece of rock crystal, probably made in the 10th century in Egypt and imported to the Rhineland via Spain, a large iron key that may have fitted a door of the synagogue, a late medieval gold ring found in the layer of rubble created by the pogrom of 1349, a child's rattle of beads inside a pottery vessel, a fragment of a floor tile depicting a leaping deer, part of a bronze Hanukkah lamp and a stylus used for writing on wax tablets. The most precious item is an earring of very high quality. Made from gold with pearls, turquoise, red glass and a Roman cut gem, it is 3.5 cm wide and was probably made in Byzantium in the late 10th or early 11th century. It was 200 or 300 years old when it fell into the latrine of a house in the goldsmiths' quarter.

Insights into Jewish life in past centuries are provided by slates on which texts were written in Hebrew, Old Yiddish and the German dialect spoken in Cologne at that time, using both the Hebrew and Latin alphabets. 400 slates were found during the excavations, mostly in the layer of burning and damage from the pogrom of 1349. Some were used to practice writing, some bear financial accounts, drawings and lists of names, others have longer texts, including extracts in verse from a tale of knights' adventures.

An inscription on a stone lintel at the side of a latrine surprised the experts on Jewish history. It says in Hebrew letters, "This is the window for removing the excrement." When a latrine was full, it had to be emptied. This one was unusually large and six metres deep, so if a long period had passed since the last time it was emptied, the occupants might have forgotten where to open it. Hebrew inscriptions in stone were normally reserved for sacred purposes, but this seems to have been an exception!

GALERIA, SCHILDERGASSE ⑧

View of the Tietz department stores', 1914

➡ From the MiQua turn into the street Obenmarspforten (the Farina perfume shop is on the corner), then take the first street on the left and follow it to Gürzenichstrasse. Walking a few steps to the right here, you will see the imposing stone façade of the Galeria department store. It was originally called *Kaufhaus Tietz*, one of many stores founded by the Jewish businessman Leonhard Tietz (1849–1914). Tietz's first shop in the Hohe Strasse in Cologne opened in 1891 and was so successful that he moved and expanded twice within ten years, building a splendid new store and arcade in the fashionable art nouveau style with stained glass, decorative gilded ironwork and the latest technology – lifts and electric lighting – from 1898 onwards. In 1914 it was replaced by the present huge building. In the same year, Leonhard Tietz died and his son Alfred took over the company.

After the National Socialists took power, they made life increasingly difficult for Jewish-owned businesses, which were "Arianised", i.e. handed to non-Jewish owners, often for a fraction of their true value. As the Tietz family were especially prominent, they had been the objects of a campaign of defamation for years already, and were forced out in 1933. The department stores were renamed as Kaufhof. Alfred Tietz and his wife Margaret emigrated to Palestine. Alfred died in Jerusalem in 1941. The family was compensated in 1951.

INFORMATION

⊙ Hohe Straße 41–53
🌐 www.galeria.de/filialen/l/koln/
hohe-strasse-41-53/001309

MY FATHER'S HOUSE

Artur Joseph, the last owner of the family shoe business (→ p. 38), emigrated to Palestine and wrote a moving book, ***Meines Vaters Haus*** (My Father's House), describing what it was like in the years of Nazi rule to be a Jew, fully integrated and well-respected in Cologne society, who regarded himself as a patriotic German and then found himself rejected and persecuted in the home town that he loved.

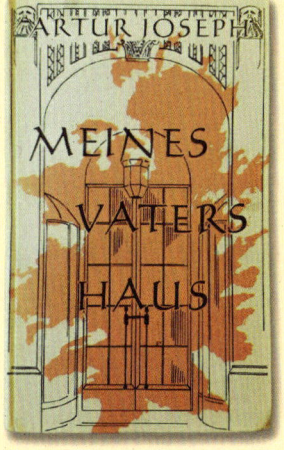

Artur Joseph fought in the German army in the First World War. Schuhhaus Joseph was the leading shoe shop in Cologne. Artur loved his native city and participated actively in Carnival celebrations. He describes visits to his grandmother, who lived over the shop. On the other side of her kitchen wall was the organ of St Anthony's Church: "As a child I often sat there and listened to the hymns and fugues coming over the stove. Later, when I sat in the office one floor further down, the sounds of the organ drifted across my desk."

Artur's memoirs, published in 1959, conclude with the words, "I love my home town ('Vaterstadt'). When I wake in the morning I think of the cathedral, of the city on the river, of how everything once was. My home. I still sense it through the cloud of smoke."

ANTONITERKIRCHE ⑨

➡ Walk west along Schildergasse, a pedestrian shopping street, until you come to a church on your left. It is dedicated to St Anthony the Hermit and was consecrated in 1384. It was the first Protestant church in Cologne: after the occupation of the Rhineland by French armies in 1794, religious toleration was introduced – Protestants were allowed to worship openly in the city for the first time, and Jews could live in Cologne again after an absence of almost 400 years.

A Stolperstein in the paving commemorates *Mathilde Joseph* (1865–1942). Here the Joseph family had a shoe shop, Schuhhaus Joseph, which was not rebuilt after its destruction in the Second World War. The business, founded by Abraham Moses Joseph in 1872, passed to his son Adolf and then in 1928 to his grandson Artur, who was forced to sell the shop in 1938. Artur Joseph's aunt Mathilde lived above the shop in the 1930s. She did not emigrate, but jumped out of the window to her death rather than face deportation to the ghetto in Theresienstadt.

INFORMATION

⊙ Schildergasse 57
🌐 antonitercitykirche.de

DISCHHAUS ⑩

From the church cross to the other side of Schildergasse and follow Herzogstrasse until you see on the right, at the corner with Glockengasse/Brückenstrasse, a building with a rounded façade. This is the Dischhaus, an early example of Modernist architecture in Cologne dating from 1930. It was originally an office building

in which some Jewish-owned companies and the chambers of Jewish lawyers were based. From 1933 until 1938 it housed the headquarter of a Jewish cultural association for the region, the Jüdischer Kulturbund Rhein-Ruhr.

In 1933 the National Socialist government excluded Jews from German cultural life. They were dismissed from theatres, opera houses, orchestras and museums. Artists were prevented from exhibiting their works. Actors, singers, musicians and performers of all kinds lost their jobs. Jews across Germany then resorted to self-help: they held concerts, film shows, talks and theatrical performances by Jewish artists for Jewish audiences. In the Rhineland and Ruhr region, this was organised by the Jüdischer Kulturbund Rhein-Ruhr – under strict supervision by the Nazi authorities. From the mid-1930s these events had to take place in the premises of Jewish institutions. After 1938 the Kulturbund was merged in a central organisation, and few Jewish cultural activities could take place at all.

⊙ Brückenstraße 19

Have a break

The ground floor of the Dischhaus is occupied by **Manufactum**, a store specialising in long-lasting, sustainable products. The coffee, cakes and light meals served here are not the cheapest in the city, but the quality is good, and the tables inside and out are a pleasant spot to relax with a drink or a snack.

⊙ Brückenstraße 23
⊙ café Mon–Fri 10am–5.30pm, Sat 10am–6pm
⊕ www.manufactum.de

STADTMUSEUM ⑪

This tour ends with a museum visit, but dedicated lovers of exhibitions will also enjoy a short diversion to the Kölnisches Stadtmuseum, which has a several displays about the city's Jewish past. The museum opened here in 2024 with modern, interactive, multi-media exhibits that provide an entertaining overview of 2,000 years of Cologne history.

You can see fragments of the bimah from the medieval synagogue (see p. 36), Jewish ritual items such as adornments of the Torah scrolls and a hanukkah lamp, evidence of pogroms such as Torah pieces from the synagogue devastated in 1938, and read about the life stories of Jews who were murdered or emigrated in the Nazi years.

To take this detour, from the Dischhaus follow Kolumbastrasse, the continuation of Herzogstrasse, and take the first right into Minoritenstrasse, where you will see the Stadtmuseum on the right.

(see p. 36)

INFORMATION

⊙ Minoritenstrasse 11
⊙ Tue-Sun 10am-5pm,
   1st Thu of the month 10am-10pm
⊕ www.koelnisches-stadtmuseum.de

Jacques Offenbach.

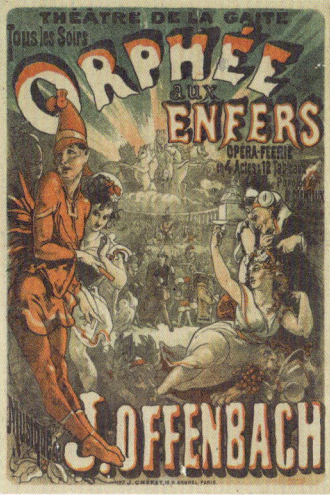

OFFENBACHPLATZ ⑫

The Dischhaus stands at the east end of Glockengasse, which is bisected by a busy six-lane road.

➜ Cross this road and walk to the left. Since 1957 the open space in front of the opera house has been called Offenbachplatz, after the composer *Jacques Offenbach*, whose statue we saw on the city hall tower. Offenbach's best-known piece is the can-can music from the operetta Orpheus in the Underworld.

In the 19th and 20th centuries, Jewish musicians played an important part in the cultural life of the city. Otto Klemperer, one of the greatest interpreters of classical music in modern times, was conductor and later musical director at the city opera house from 1917 until 1924. The tradition lives on in Cologne's Shalom music festival, featuring works and performances by Jewish composers and musicians

🌐 www.shalom-musik.koeln

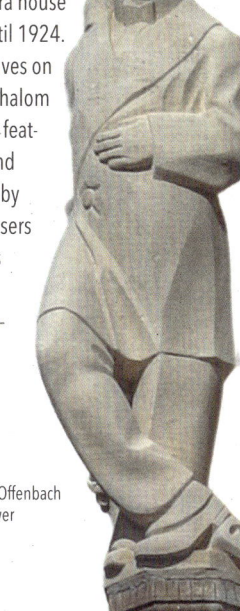
Statue of Jacques Offenbach on the city hall tower

GLOCKENGASSE ⑬

A plaque on the north wall of the opera house commemorates the synagogue that once stood close to this spot.

In 1801, three years after Jews were allowed to settle in Cologne for the first time since 1424, a Jewish congregation was re-established in the city, occupying buildings in Glockengasse that had belonged to a nuns' convent. This was the place of work of Isaac Offenbach, the father of Jacques. The community was too small and poor in its first years to build a synagogue or employ a rabbi, but had school rooms and accommodation for employees, and a prayer hall holding about 120 persons.

As the community grew in numbers and wealth, the banker Abraham Oppenheim paid for a new synagogue on the site, completed in 1861. The cathedral architect Ernst Friedrich Zwirner designed a tall domed building in the Moorish style. The choice of an Islamic style with minaret-like turrets may seem strange, but it was considered to reflect the Middle Eastern origins of Judaism and distinguished the building architecturally from Christian churches. Tall windows beneath the dome bathed the interior in light. The walls were brightly decorated in blue, red and gold, contrasting with the white marble of the Torah ark.

The synagogue burned during the November pogrom of 1938, and its remains were cleared a few years later.

Cologne, synagogue in Glockengasse, print of a lithograph after a drawing by Peter Parrit (19th century)

CLOSE UP

ABRAHAM OPPENHEIM

Abraham Freiherr von Oppenheim
(1804-1878)

The most prominent Jewish citizen of Cologne in the 19th century (1804-78) was the son of the banker Salomon Oppenheim. Abraham and his brother Simon managed the family bank with great success and were leading investors in the railway, insurance and shipping business, making a significant contribution to the economy of the Rhineland. Abraham showed his civic commitment by campaigning for equal rights for Jews and became the first Jewish member of Cologne's city council. He not only financed the synagogue but was also one of the leading donors for the completion of Cologne Cathedral. He was the first Jew to be ennobled by the Prussian state: Baron Abraham von Oppenheim. After his death, his wife Charlotte preserved his memory by founding a children's hospital and donating the Oppenheim Window in the cathedral (→ p. 20). The family bank, Sal. Oppenheim and Co., with a sixth-generation Oppenheim in control until 2005, prospered until the financial crisis of 2009-10, when it was taken over by Deutsche Bank.

LAW COURTS ⑭

From Glockengasse, Schwertnergasse and its continuation lead north. We pass beneath the tall building of the public broadcaster WDR and see a three-storey building of red brick with stone facings around the windows and the corners. These are the law courts, where in the 1930s many cases were heard under the Nuremberg Laws of 1935. These laws excluded Jews from German citizenship, removed the full civic rights that Jews had enjoyed since 1871, and forbade marriage and sexual relations between non-Jewish people and Jews. Prosecutions in these law courts resulted in the imprisonment of persons who failed to comply with the Nuremberg Laws.

By contrast, in 1979 the law courts were the scene of the trial of an old Nazi. Kurt Lischka, a lawyer who joined the SS, was head of the Gestapo in Cologne in 1940, and later commanded the German security service in occupied Paris. He was instrumental in deporting tens of thousands of French Jews. Although French courts sentenced him to life imprisonment in his absence, he lived in freedom in Cologne until his arrest in 1979, following a campaign by the French Nazi-hunter Serge Klarsfeld and his German wife Beate. Lischka was sentenced to ten years in prison, released on health grounds in 1985, and died in his eightieth year in 1989.

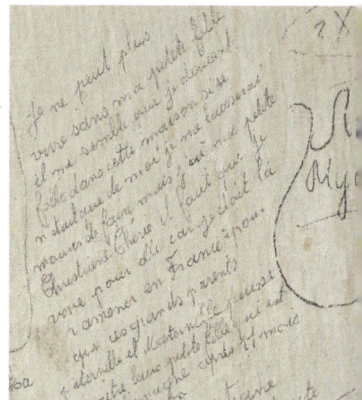

The documentation and exhibition centre dedicated to the victims of persecution by the National Socialists is housed in the EL-DE-Haus, a building that was used for ten years as the Cologne headquarter of the Nazi secret police, the Gestapo. The Gestapo was behind the pogrom of November 1939 and was responsible for organising the deportation of Jews to the death camps. The cellars of the EL-DE-Haus were used as cells. Political opponents of the Nazis from the Communist and Social Democratic Parties, forced labourers from many European countries and Jews were imprisoned, interrogated and tortured here. More than 400 were executed, usually by hanging, in the back yard.

Visitors can see graffiti scratched into the walls of the cellars in German, Polish, Russian, Ukrainian, Dutch, French and Italian, and view an extensive exhibition on the first and second floors on the events leading to the Nazi seizure of power and the years 1933 to 1945. The fate of Cologne's Jews is documented in detail, with maps of Jewish institutions in the city and the routes of deportation, the last letters written by deported persons to their relatives, individual life stories, and a copy of the Gedenkbuch, "Book of Memorial", listing thousands of Jews who lived in Cologne.

The NS-DOK continues its research to preserve the memory of victims of persecution and does educational work so that the crimes of the National Socialists will not be forgotten or denied. The website and the audio-guide to the exhibition are available in the following languages: German, English, Hebrew, French, Dutch, Spanish, Russian and Polish.

If you still have time and energy after visiting NS-DOK, it takes only five minutes to walk to the monument to Edith Stein (Gereonstrasse 12) or the Yavne Memorial Centre (→ p. 56).

(→ p. 56)

INFORMATION

⊙ Appellhofplatz 23–25
⊙ Tue–Fri 10am–6pm, Sat, Sun 11am–6pm
⊕ www.nsdok.de

EDITH STEIN

A striking work of art stands in front of the archbishop's residence on Gereon-strasse. It commemorates a Jewish German philosopher who became a Roman Catholic nun and depicts the duality of Edith Stein's life: a Jewish path, illustrated by tablets of the ten commandments and the motif of piles of empty shoes, a reference to the Holocaust, and the Christian path of a Carmelite nun.

She was born in Breslau (now Wroclaw in Poland) in 1891 and studied there before taking a doctorate at Freiburg University. In 1922 she converted to Catholicism and spent the following years writing and lecturing on philosophy. Forced out of teaching in 1933, she entered the Carmelite monastery in Cologne, taking the name Teresa Benedicta of the Cross. Under the threat of persecution, she and her sister Rosa, also a convert, moved to a Carmelite house in the Netherlands, where they were arrested in 1942 and sent to die in the gas chamber in Birkenau. Edith Stein was beatified in 1987 by Pope John Paul II during his visit to Cologne and later canonised.

FROM NEUMARKT TO YAVNE

1. Bodenheimer memorial plaque
2. Gesundheitsamt
3. Kunsthaus Lempertz
4. Central City Library: Germania Judaica
5. Griechenmarktviertel
6. Konrad Adenauer
7. Yavne Education and Memorial Centre
🍴 Törtchen Törtchen

A CITY WALK

Around Neumarkt, a large square and traffic hub in the city centre, are a number of places with associations to the story of the Jewish community in modern times.

MAX BODENHEIMER ①

➡ In Richmodstrasse, the side street in the middle of the north side of Neumarkt, walk beneath the tall stone tower with two horses' heads and look out for a memorial plaque with a Star of David set into the paving. The design for the flag of the state of Israel originated in this building. The plaque marks the site of the office of **Max Bodenheimer**, a leading light of the Zionist movement, with the following words: "In 1899 in this house Dr Max Bodenheimer conceived the idea of an organization for the establishment of a Jewish state – Israel" and quotes Bodenheimer's description of his vision: "A heavenly call rang in my ears: save your people, lest it die!". From 1905 onwards Bodenheimer was director of the Jewish National Fund (JNF) and organised from his office here the financing of land purchases in Palestine. For example, in 1909 the JNF enabled Jewish families from overcrowded Jaffa to buy land to the north of the city, a purchase that is regarded as the foundation of Tel Aviv.

STÄDTISCHES GESUNDHEITSAMT ②

Since 1940 the building with the stone façade on the south side of Neumarkt (at its eastern end) has been the *Gesundheitsamt*, the municipal health department. It was constructed in 1909 as the company headquarters of the Jewish Bing family, who traded in high-quality textiles. They were forced to sell the building to the city authorities in 1939 at a price far below its true value. In 1930, 150 Jewish doctors worked in the city, 15% of the total, but from 1938 those who remained were only allowed to treat Jewish patients and excluded from all other activities. This persecution, and other crimes of the Nazi authorities such as forced sterilisation, was organised from this building by the Gesundheitsamt. The heirs of the Bing family received compensation in 1952. A plaque on the right-hand wall of the lobby records what happened here in the years 1940 to 1945.

CLOSE UP

THE COLOGNE THESES

In 1896 Max Isidor Bodenheimer, David Wolffsohn and Moritz Levy published the Cologne Theses, which were adopted by the First Zionist Congress in Basel the following year and thus were a basis for founding the state of Israel in 1948. The first thesis: "Bound together by common ancestry and shared history, the Jews of all countries constitute a national community." Secondly: "History shows that the civil emancipation of Jews as citizens of other countries is insufficient to ensure the social and cultural future of the Jewish people." Bodenheimer concluded that the only solution was to create a Jewish national state in the "historically sacred ground of Palestine", and to this end called for support of Jewish colonies there, for the cultivation of Jewish culture, customs and language, and for the establishment of Zionist associations in all German cities. Bodenheimer's close associate in Cologne was David Wolffsohn, who succeeded Theodor Herzl as president of the World Zionist Organization in 1905.

A HEAVENLY CALL RANG IN MY EARS·SAVE

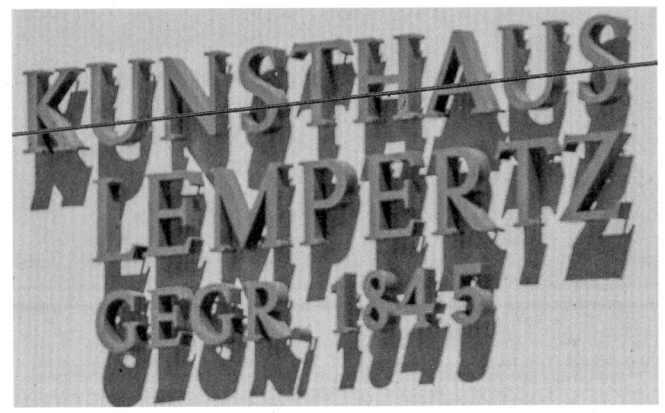

KUNSTHAUS LEMPERTZ ③

Diagonally opposite the Gesundheits-amt, on a corner of the east side of Neumarkt, is **Kunsthaus Lempertz**, a highly respected auction house for art. In 1939 an auction of "non-Aryan property" was held here: paintings, sculptures and oriental carpets belonging to Walter Westfeld, a Jewish art critic and gallery owner, who was forced to abandon his gallery in the city of Wuppertal in 1936. He moved to Düsseldorf, where he and his non-Jewish wife were prosecuted under the Nazi race laws for the "crime" of living together. Westfeld succeeded in smuggling some of his art to France, but the rest, including paintings by Rubens, Böcklin, Pissaro and von Lenbach, was confiscated. Westfeld was forced to work on the catalogue for the auction, arrested and imprisoned under currency laws, then deported to Theresienstadt and to Auschwitz, where he was murdered in 1943. His heirs have been able to recover only a few of the auctioned works. In 2009 the Staatsgalerie in Stuttgart returned two 19th-century paintings, and in 2011 the Museum of Fine Arts in Boston gave compensation for a 17th-century Portrait of a Man and Woman by the Dutch artist van der Neer.

CENTRAL CITY LIBRARY ④

Josef-Haubrich-Hof across the road and to the south of Kunsthaus Lempertz is the site of the **central city library** (currently closed for renovation). The library houses an important collection of written materials, **Germania Judaica**. This institution was founded in 1959 by a group of committed persons including Heinrich Böll, a native of Cologne and winner of the Nobel Prize for Literature in 1972, in the belief that "ignorance promotes prejudice". Their aim was to raise public awareness about the history of Judaism in Germany and combat the anti-Semitism that still existed: in the late 1950s, among other anti-Jewish incidents, swastikas were daubed on the synagogues in Cologne and Düsseldorf.

The Germania Judaica collection of 90,000 books and a huge number of newspapers, journals and magazines is

The first issue of the Bulletin of Germania Judaica (1960/61, Germania Judaica)

Dr Jutta Bohnke-Kollwitz in conversation with Heinrich Böll at the Germania Judaica collection

thought to be the largest of its kind in Europe. Jewish history and culture in Germany and in general, biographies, Jewish literary works, graphic novels, and books about anti-Semitism past and present, as well as studies of the Zionist movement and the situation in Israel and neighbouring regions today are included in the holdings.

INFORMATION

⊙ During the renovation work from 2026:
   Hohe Straße 68–82

🌐 germaniajudaica.de

GRIECHENMARKTVIERTEL ⑤

The district to the south of Neumarkt is called the *Griechenmarktviertel*. In the 19th and early 20th century, this quarter was home to many poor Jews who had fled from persecution in eastern Europe. The housing here was severely damaged in bombing during the Second World War, and few original buildings stand as witnesses to the Jewish community – but some powerful memories remain of what once happened here (see opposite page).

the Federal Republic of Germany (1949–63). Adenauer had lifelong sympathy for Jewish causes: he had Jewish school friends, was a member of the Pro-Palestine Committee in the 1920s, and in the face of domestic opposition signed the Reparations Agreement between Israel and Germany. He encouraged the return of Jews to Germany, was instrumental in the reconstruction of the synagogue in Cologne, had an excellent relationship with David Ben-Gurion, the first Israeli prime minister, and visited Israel in 1966.

KONRAD ADENAUER ⑥

At the west end of Neumarkt stands the church St. Aposteln. In front of its north wall is a statue of *Konrad Adenauer*, mayor of Cologne (1917–33) and first chancellor of

➜ From here walk along Apostelnstrasse and St.-Apern-Strasse, then turn left into Helenenstrasse.

Have a
break

Törtchen Törtchen has exquisite patisserie products – cakes, macarons, and small hand-made tarts that are true works of art. The café is also open for a more hearty brunch or lunch.

⚲ Apostelnstraße 19
◷ Mon–Sat 9am–6pm, Sun 10am–6pm
⊕ toertchentoertchen.de

CLOSE UP

A BRAVE MAN – RICHARD STERN

Richard Stern, wearing the Iron Cross awarded to him in the First World War, in front of his shop at Marsilstein 20

Richard Stern, born in 1899, fought with the German army in the First World War and was awarded the Iron Cross "for courage in the face of the enemy". He later took over the family shop selling bedlinen, pillows and cushions at Marsilstein no. 20 in the Griechenmarktviertel. Like other Jewish businesses, it was targeted in the boycott of 1 April 1933. A photograph taken on that day shows Richard Stern wearing his Iron Cross, standing in the door of the shop next to a stormtrooper in Nazi uniform with a swastika armband. Stern had printed a flyer addressed "To all comrades from the front and Germans", in which he pointed out that 12,000 Jewish German soldiers died in the First World War, that Reich ministers Göring and Frick had declared that insulting soldiers who had fought at the front was punishable by imprisonment, and that the boycott was an affront to loyal Jewish German citizens. In the pogrom night in November 1938 he went into hiding to avoid arrest, emigrated to America – and returned to Europe in 1945 as a soldier in the US Army. He died in the USA in 1967.

YAVNE EDUCATION AND MEMORIAL CENTRE ⑦

On the small open space called Erich-Klibansky-Platz stands a fountain crowned by a lion that stands upright, roaring from wide-open jaws and pointing its sharp claws to the sky. It holds a tablet of the laws in Hebrew script. This is the lion of Juda, a symbol of the Jewish people, and the octagonal fountain is a memorial for 1,100 Jewish children of Cologne who were murdered in the Holocaust. Their names are engraved around the fountain basin, behind which is the *Yavne Education and Memorial Centre*.

A plaque on a wall nearby records that the synagogue of Adass Jeschurun, the orthodox "community of Israel", stood here from 1884. Along with the adjoining teachers' college and the Yavne high school, it was destroyed in the pogrom of 1938 and a later bombing raid. Until 1933 the pupils came mainly from orthodox eastern European families. Later, as Jews were increasingly excluded from the life of the city, liberal families too sent their children here.

The Yavne Memorial Centre has a moving exhibition about the Adass Jeschurun community and the school, and holds talks and events on related subjects. The lion of Juda on the fountain is the work of Hermann Gurfinkel, who was a pupil at the Yavne school.

INFORMATION

⊙ Erich-Klibansky-Platz 7,
   Access via Helenenstrasse
⊙ Tue–Thu 11am–2pm, Thu also 4–7pm,
   Sun 12–4pm
⊕ www.jawne.de

CLOSE UP

ERICH KLIBANSKY AND THE KINDERTRANSPORT

To prepare pupils of the Yavne school for emigration, lessons about Palestine and the English language were introduced. The school director, Dr Erich Klibansky, planned to transfer the entire school to England and personally travelled to London in 1939, sending 130 children in four groups. This was part of the Kindertransport, through which the United Kingdom agreed to take Jewish children from Nazi Germany in 1938–39. About 10,000 made the journey, separated from parents whom most never saw again, carrying only a single suitcase. They took trains to the Netherlands and crossed the sea to Harwich, arriving in London at Liverpool Street Station, where there is a memorial.

Erich Klibansky returned from England and was unable to save himself and his own family. With his wife and three sons, he was deported to Minsk and murdered there in 1942. The life stories of children who went to England on the Kindertransport are described in English here: ***www.kindertransporte-nrw.eu***. A powerful account of experiences in the Kindertransport is given in English by Schmuel Hatsor: ***www.jawne.de/en/kindertransport***

NEUSTADT AND SYNAGOGUE

① Rathenauplatz
② Synagoge
③ Boisseréestrasse
④ Lochnerstrasse

⑤ Meister-Gerhard-Strasse
⑥ Yitzhak-Rabin-Platz

🍴 Café Fleur

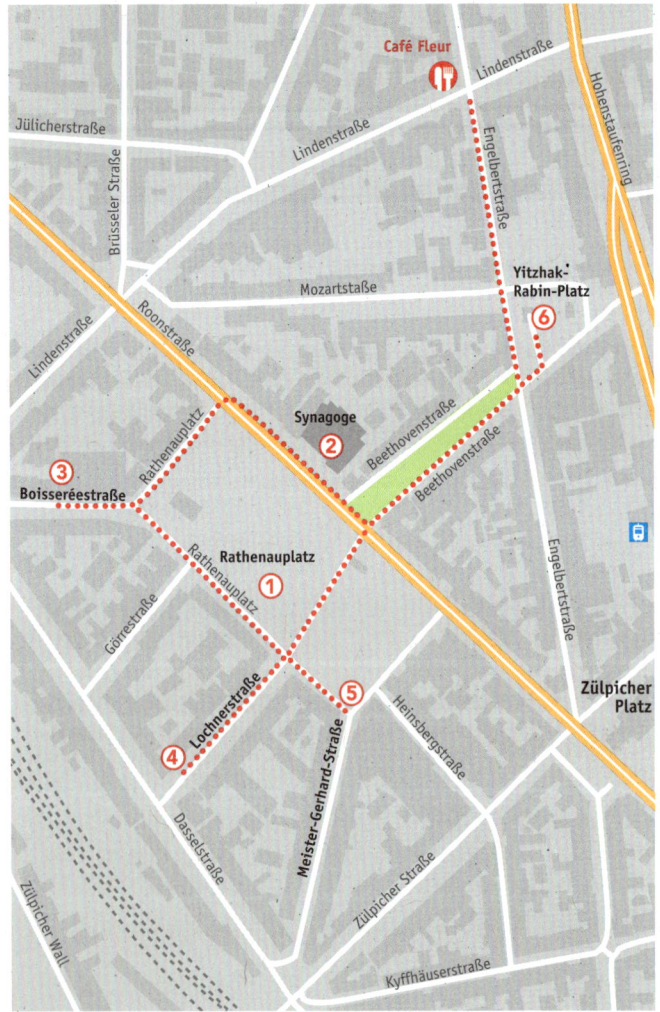

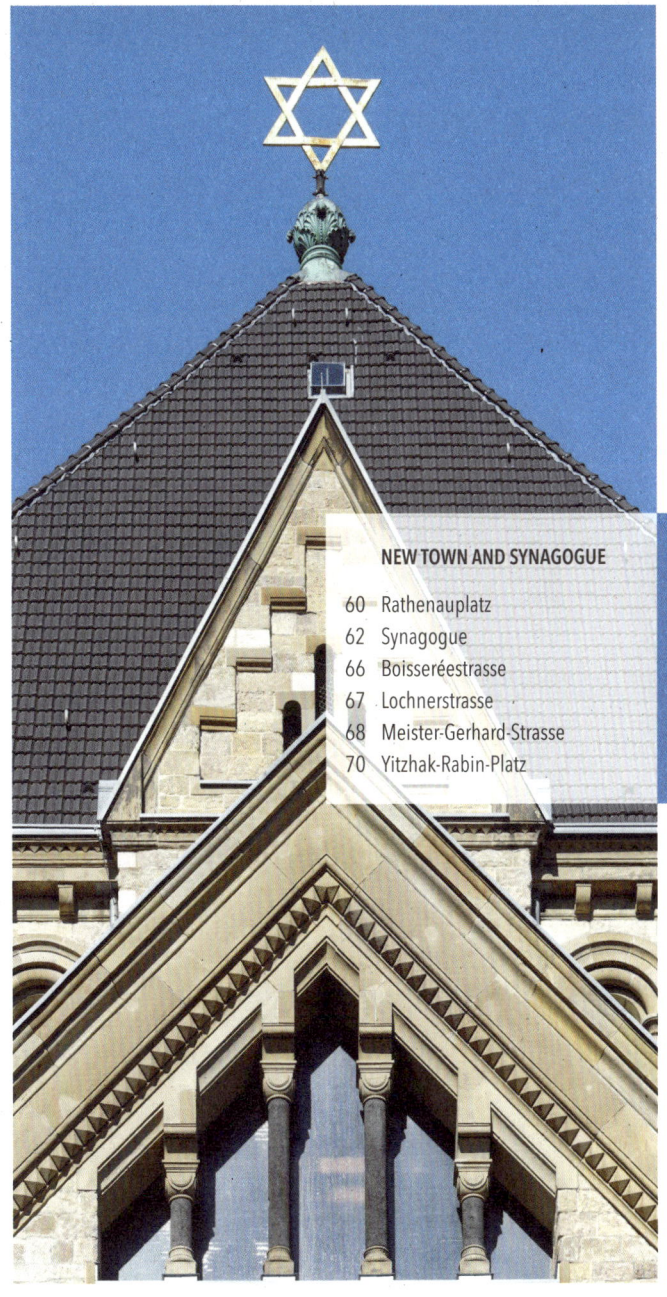

NEW TOWN AND SYNAGOGUE

THE NEW TOWN AND SYNAGOGUE

This exploration of Jewish life in Cologne's New Town begins at Rathenauplatz. Walk there from Neumarkt (just over 1 kilometre, 15 minutes), or take a tram to Rudolfplatz (lines 1, 7, 12, 15) or Zülpicher Platz (lines 9, 12, 15).

RATHENAUPLATZ ①

The synagogue stands on one of the most attractive squares in Cologne. Rathenauplatz, with sports facilities and children's playground, benches beneath shady plane trees and a beer garden, is screened from the roaring traffic of Roonstrasse. The square takes its name from a Jewish industrialist and politician, Walther Rathenau (1867–1922), who was murdered by right-wing nationalists. His father, Emil Rathenau, founded a large electrical company, AEG. Walther was chairman of the supervisory board of AEG and one of the principal organisers of the German war economy during the First World War. In 1922 he became foreign minister and negotiated the Treaty of Rapallo, which established relations between Germany

regarded him as a traitorous member of a Jewish Communist conspiracy. A paramilitary group assassinated him.

Rathenauplatz was laid out in the late 19th century as part of the Neustadt, the New Town, outside the medieval city walls. Along the semi-circle of old fortifications arose a broad avenue of fine residences designed in various historical styles: the Ring. Parks, open spaces, and roads radiating outwards with views of carefully placed churches and public buildings such as the opera house made the Ring and the areas beyond it a desirable place to live. In keeping with this status, the original name of Rathenauplatz was Königsplatz, King Square. From 1933 to 1945 it was called Horst-Wessel-Platz after a "martyr" of the Nazi Party who was killed in street fighting.

Dr. Walter Rathenau

and Soviet Russia. For this, and for his insistence that Germany fulfil the obligations imposed by the Treaty of Versailles in 1919, ultra-nationalists

SYNAGOGUE – THEN AND NOW ②

Many aspiring middle-class Jews came to live and work in the New Town. This made the location of the synagogue, inaugurated in 1899, both prestigious and convenient. The synagogue in Glockengasse was too small for the growing Jewish community, which was also increasingly diverse – whereas Orthodox Jews had established facilities in St-Apern-Strasse, here the synagogue served the needs of a liberal congregation, which financed the imposing building almost entirely from its own means.

The neo-Romanesque architectural style was chosen. Viewed from the park today, the façade closely resembles its original appearance with its large rose window, behind which rise a pyramidal roof and two pointed turrets. Flanking the central block to left and right were meeting rooms, school rooms, offices and apartments for rabbis, etc. The interior, which seated 800 men beneath a dome in the centre and 600 women in galleries, was fitted out opulently with white marble, painted deco-

rations and a Torah ark made from mahogany. In accordance with liberal religious practice, the bimah for Torah readings was placed near to the ark rather than at the centre of the hall – and in 1906 an organ was installed, an addition that the orthodox vehemently rejected. The complex also included a mikveh, a smaller synagogue space and a prayer room for ortho-dox Jews.

In November 1938 a mob set fire to the synagogue and desecrated its sacred artefacts. In 1941 the buildings housed Jewish citizens, including the last pre-war rabbi, who had been forcibly removed from their homes. The complex suffered further damage from Allied bombs. In April 1945 a small number of surviving Jews held a religious service in the ruins of the building. As a Jewish community reassembled in the post-war years, the project of restoring the synagogue gained support. Its protagonists included Konrad Adenauer, the first post-war chancellor of the Federal Republic of Germany, who had been mayor of Cologne from 1917 until 1933. The architect for rebuilding was *Helmut Goldschmidt* (1918–2005), son of a Jewish father and a Roman Catholic mother, who also restored synagogues in several other cities, including Bonn and Dortmund.

Goldschmidt made one major change to the interior. He divided the central hall into two levels, with a large room for community events below and the hall for worship, reduced in height, above. The building reopened in 1959. In place of the elaborate decoration of the original, today the interior has a plainer but – thanks to beautiful stained-glass windows – not austere style. In the same year, two young German members of an extreme right-wing nationalist party painted a Nazi swastika and anti-Jewish slogans on the wall of the synagogue, an outrage that prompted the head of the Cologne city education department, who was visiting Israel at the time, to contact his counterpart in Tel Aviv. This resulted in an exchange of school students, which continues to this day.

From 1953 to 1965 the official mission of the state of Israel to the Federal Republic of Germany was based in the synagogue premises. Visitors today see a memorial room and an exhibition on the history of the building and the community.

INFORMATION

⊙ Roonstrasse 50 (on the square Rathenauplatz)

⊕ www.sgk.de

A BIRTHPLACE OF ZIONISM

Moses Hess   Max Isidor Bodenheimer   David Wolffsohn

Among the founding fathers of Zionism – the movement to establish a Jewish state in Palestine – were three men who lived and worked in Cologne. **Moses Hess** (→ p. 28) was an early advocate of a Jewish national state in his book Rome and Jerusalem, published in 1862. In the later 19th century, pogroms in eastern Europe and anti-Semitism in German society drove the movement. The lawyer **Max Isidor Bodenheimer** (1865–1940) founded a Zionist association in Cologne in 1893. Bodenheimer was the first president of the Zionist Federation of Germany. In 1933 he emigrated to Palestine and, like Moses Hess, is commemorated with a statue on the city hall tower. His collaborator **David Wolffsohn** (1855–1914), who succeeded Theodor Herzl as president of the World Zionist Organisation, was buried in the Jewish cemetery in Deutz, and reinterred in 1952 in Jerusalem next to Herzl's grave. The activities of Bodenheimer and Wolffsohn were not appreciated by all Jews: some who identified as patriotic Germans regarded Zionism as unhelpful for their harmonious assimilation into society.

Town hall tower, Moses Hess

BOISSERÉESTRASSE ③

A stroll around Rathenauplatz still conveys an impression of the residential streets that constituted the Neustadt in the late 19th century. In front of Boisseréestrasse no. 3 are Stolpersteine for three members of the Friedemann family, who were deported to Minsk and murdered there in 1942, and for Betty and Hermann Simchowitz. High-status residents of such houses lived in large apartments with high ceilings on the mezzanine or first floor, while the less wealthy occupied the rooms higher up, or some-

times in a second building behind the back yard. The Simchowitz family were prosperous. Betty's husband Sascha (1865–1930), a doctor who had his practice in the house, was also an acknowledged scholar of literature who directed plays in Cologne theatres. Their son Hermann, also a doctor, worked in a hospital until he was forced out in 1933. Then he too installed his medical practice in Boisseréestrasse. Hermann emigrated to the USA in 1937, but his mother was deported and died in the Theresienstadt ghetto in 1942.

LOCHNERSTRASSE ④

➡ Walk along the south-west side of Rathenauplatz and turn right into Lochnerstrasse. In the primary school on the left, no. 13–15, heartbreaking scenes took place on 28 October 1938. Jews who had Polish citizenship were deported on that date. They were given only a few hours' notice to gather belongings, told to assemble in the school yard here, and then taken by train to the Polish border.

House no. 12–14 opposite the school was the home of Dr Isidor Caro and his wife Klara. Isidor came to Cologne in 1908 and was the last pre-war rabbi in the nearby synagogue. Klara was an energetic and committed member of the community (→ p. 62). In 1942 the couple were deported to Theresienstadt, where Isidor died. Klara survived and lived in the USA until her death in 1979.

DR. ISIDOR CARO
JG. 1876
LEHRTE AM
GYMNASIUM KREUZGASSE
DEPORTIERT 1942
THERESIENSTADT
VERHUNGERT 1943

MEISTER-GERHARD-STRASSE ⑤

➡ Walk back to Rathenauplatz and turn right, then right again into Meister-Gerhard-Strasse. In front of number 5 on the opposite side of the street, four more Stolpersteine have been set into the pavement, commemorating Hans David Tobar, his wife Ursel and their children Theo and Lilo. Hans David Tobar was a well-known and successful entertainer, especially at Carnival celebrations in Cologne. From 1933 onwards he was forbidden to perform in public. In 1939 he emigrated with Ursel and the children to New York, where he died in 1956. In New York he founded a Carnival association for exiled Germans – he was a born showman with the typical mentality of Rhinelanders, who love merry performances and laughter.

CLOSE UP

JEWISH CITIZENS AND CARNIVAL

The Small Council of the K.K.K., 1920s (photo from the estate of Max Salomon, Los Angeles/USA)

It is hard to overstate the importance of Carnival in Cologne. In other parts of the world, events are limited to the days before Ash Wednesday, especially Mardi Gras/Shrove Tuesday. In the Rhineland, uninhibited revelry on the streets and in pubs goes on for six days, starting on the Thursday before Ash Wednesday – but in addition, these celebrations in public are preceded by months of shows, meetings and parties behind closed doors. Many locals are members of Carnival associations who spend much of the year preparing costumes and practising for parades and performances. For Jews who were well integrated or assimilated into German society, to join whole-heartedly in this central event in the life of their city was and is the most natural thing in the world.

When the big parade on Carnival Monday was held for only the second time in 1824, the part of one of its leading figures, Princess Venetia, was taken by Simon Oppenheim from the Jewish banking family. At Artur Joseph's shoe store (→ p. 37), the shop windows were cleared out so that the family could cheer the parade with 300 customers. A number of Jewish entertainers performed at Carnival shows, most notably Hans David Tobar (→ p. 68), and there was a Jewish Carnival society, called the Kleiner Kölner Klub. This ended abruptly, however, with the Nazi takeover of power in 1933. From that time onwards, the themed floats in the Carnival parades displayed anti-Semitic motifs.

In 2017 a Jewish Carnival society was founded again, the ***Kölsche Kippa Köpp – KKK***, recalling the Kleiner Kölner Klub of the 1920s. The Carnival society named StattGarde Colonia Ahoj awards the Hans David Tobar Prize to a person who has shown commitment to the acceptance of minority groups. In 2024, the City of Cologne invited the grand-daughter of Hans Tobar to come from the USA to watch the celebrations and see an exhibition at the NS-DOK centre about Jewish participation in Carnival.

YITZHAK-RABIN-PLATZ ⑥

➡ To end this tour, cross Rathenau-platz and walk along Beethovenstrasse, which leads to the Ring. The houses that used to stand at no. 6 and 16 in Beethovenstrasse, now replaced by post-war buildings, were ghetto houses, in which Jews who had been expelled from their own homes were crowded together from 1941 onwards. The small open space at the end of Beethovenstrasse is Yitzhak-Rabin-Platz, named after the Israeli prime minister who was assassinated in 1995 by an Israeli opposed to Rabin's signing of the Oslo Accords between Israel and the Palestine Liberation Organisation. Rabin's childhood was spent in Cologne's twin city of Tel Aviv. The ceremonial naming of Yitzhak-Rabin-Platz took place in 1996 in the presence of his widow Leah.

Have a *break*

From Beethovenstrasse turn left at Yitzhak-Rabin-Platz and walk along Engelbertstrasse: **Café Fleur** is a pleasant café-bar and bistro, serving all-day breakfast and good wines, long drinks and tarte flambée in the evening.

⊙ Lindenstraße 10
⊙ Mon–Sat 9am–midnight, Sun 10am–10pm
⊕ www.cafe-fleur.de

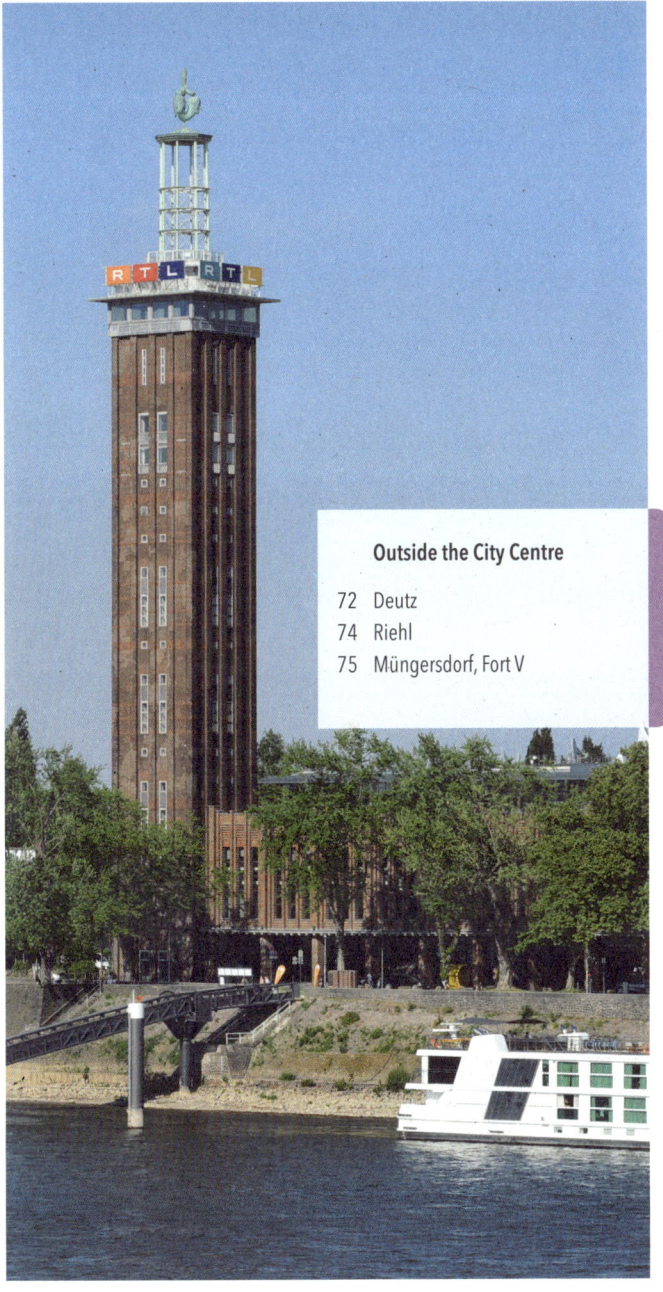

Outside the City Centre

DEUTZ

The Old Synagogue in Deutz, 1884, watercolour by Wilhelm Scheiner (1852–1922)

Deutz, the district on the east bank of the Rhine opposite the cathedral, was not incorporated into the city of Cologne until 1888. In the Middle Ages it was part of the territory controlled by the archbishop, who allowed Jews to remain there when the city authorities expelled them from the west bank of the river in 1424. It is possible that some of the Jews expelled from Cologne in 1424 simply crossed the river to Deutz, but we have no record of a Jewish community there until the 16th century. 96 persons are named in a list dating from 1596. They were not prosperous merchants, but a small Jewish community earning a modest living, for example as butchers or small traders. They were not allowed to do business across the river in Cologne, but they employed a ferryman, a Christian who took them over to the west bank, where they could trade goods without actually stepping onto dry land.

The only remains of Jewish life in Deutz today are modern memorials, and a cemetery (→ p. 82). Walk across the north side of the Hohenzollern-brücke, the railway bridge, to see on reaching the east bank brick buildings dating from the 1920s with a tower facing the river. They were built as trade-fair halls. A *monument on the north side of the tower* records the use of the halls in the Nazi years as a Gestapo labour camp, an outstation of the Buchenwald concentration camp and as a transit point for the 12,000 Cologne Jews who were put on trains in Deutz-Tief station and transported to the death camps. The furniture left behind by deported Jews was stored in the hall next to the tower and given to bombed-out families. Konrad Adenauer was interned here, as were members of the Roma and Sinti minorities who also went to their deaths from Deutz-Tief.

Further south, a road bridge, the Deutzer Brücke, leads to the street Deutzer Freiheit. Turn right here into Luisenstrasse to reach *Reischplatz*, the site of a synagogue that was set ablaze in the pogrom night of November 1938. Its predecessors stood close to the river at the west end of Deutzer Freiheit. The first of them was destroyed by flooding in 1784 and replaced by a second building, which had to make way for construction of the bridge in 1914. In 1915 a new synagogue was opened on Reischplatz with seating for 240 men and 100 women in the gallery and an apartment for the rabbi's family on the third floor. After 1938 the building was greatly altered and used as a police station until 2010. Today nothing remains to recall the former use of *Reischplatz no. 6* except Stolpersteine for the last rabbi, Julius Simons, and his wife, who were murdered in Auschwitz in 1944.

RIEHL

One of the architects of the housing estate known as the ***Naumann-siedlung*** was Manfred Faber, a protagonist of Neues Bauen (New Architecture), a movement in the early 20th century that aimed to produce desirable, practical residential buildings, well-ventilated with lots of sunlight and without the ornamented historical styles of previous generations. The housing of the Naumann Quarter, situated between Barbarastrasse and Boltensternstrasse, reflects those ideals to this day. Faber, born in 1879, was deported to Theresienstadt in 1942 and sent to die in the gas chamber at Auschwitz in 1944. A wall plaque commemorates him.

MÜNGERSDORF, FORT V

A fort built in the 1870s as part of an outer defensive ring on the western edge of the city was used as a prison camp at the start of the Second World War. From late 1942, the process began of moving the approximately 6,000 Jews who remained in Cologne in "ghetto houses" to this fort. Up to 2,500 people at any one time endured cramped and unhygienic conditions here without any heating. Many died or killed themselves before they could be deported from the fort to the death camps. The fort was demolished in 1947. A memorial stone and inscription, set up in 1981, marks Its site on Walter-Binder-Weg. Further comme-moration nearby is the installation "Wall", created by the architect and artist Simon Ungers for the Bürgerverein (citizens' association) of Müngersdorf. 19 metres wide and 4 metres tall, it consists of eight flanged steel girders into which seven windows have been cut.

INFORMATION

⊙ Walter-Binder-Weg, 50933 Köln
⊕ museenkoeln.de/NS-Dokumentations-zentrum/Gedenkort-Deportationslager-Muengersdorf

A fountain (1987) in the courtyard of the Farina-Haus featuring women of Cologne through the ages

JEWISH WOMEN

Many strong, talented Jewish women made their mark on the history of modern Cologne. Here are five of them.

Therese Oppenheim, born Deigen Levi in Dülmen, Westphalia in 1775, married the banker Salomon Oppenheim and ran the family bank on her husband's death in 1828. She gave birth to twelve children, two of whom, Abraham and Simon, later took over the banking business. She died in Cologne in 1842.

Rahel Apfel (1857–1912) was born Rahel Bürger in the town of Siegburg and married the gynaecologist Simon Apfel. In 1885 they moved to Cologne, and in 1894 bought a house at Elisenstrasse no. 15, where Rahel held a highly regarded literary salon on Friday evenings. She wrote stories and poems, and was a co-founder with Max Isidor Bodenheimer of the National Jewish Association.

Klara Caro, née Beermann, was born in Berlin in 1886 and married the rabbi Isidor Caro, who came to Cologne in 1908 (→ p. 67). As an active member of the Israelitischer Frauenverein, the Jewish women's association, she campaigned for women's rights, their education and career opportunities. From the late 1920s, hoping to counteract rising anti-Semitism, she gave courses on Jewish religion and culture. She and her husband rejected the option of emigrating in the 1930s and were taken to the Theresienstadt ghetto, where she ran a women's group and organised cultural and religious events. She survived the ghetto and died in the USA in 1979.

Hertha Kraus (1897–1968) gained a doctorate in social studies in Frankfurt. She became a Quaker, joined the Social Democratic Party, and became head of the social services department in Cologne in 1923 – the only woman to hold a leading position in the city administration. She was instrumental in setting up retirement homes in the Riehl district, which exist to this day. Dismissed in 1933 due to her Jewish heritage, she emigrated to the USA and held a professorship at Bryn Mawr College in Philadelphia. She returned many times to post-war Germany to assist in the establishment of social services. A statue on the city hall tower and the Hertha-Krauss-Strasse in Riehl honour her (→ p. 29).

Maria Herz (1878–1950), from the Bing family of textile merchants (→ p. 54), was a composer of lieder, chamber music and pieces for choir. After her marriage to Albert Herz in 1901, the couple moved to England, feeling oppressed by anti-Semitism in German society. When they returned to Cologne for a wedding in 1914, the outbreak of war forced them to stay. Her harpsichord concerto was performed in Cologne at the Shalom music festival (www.shalom-musik.koeln) in 2024 for the first time since she wrote it in 1935, a year before she emigrated to England again.

The Cologne Women's Prize, awarded since 2020 for work for the equality of women and men, is named after *Else Falk* (1872–1956), a socially committed campaigner for women's rights who, being of Jewish descent, was forced to resign from her position as chair of the women's associations in Cologne in 1933. With her husband she emigrated to Belgium in 1939, survived the war there, and spent her final years with her son in Brazil.

CLOSE UP

THE TWINNING OF COLOGNE AND TEL AVIV

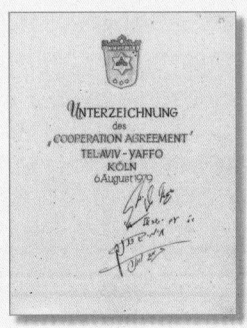

UNTERZEICHNUNG
des
, COOPERATION AGREEMENT '
TEL AVIV - YAFFO
KÖLN
6 August 1979

In 1960 a trip to Israel by 35 young people from Cologne was a political issue. Fifteen years after the Shoa, many Israelis did not want any contact with Germany. The fear that anti-Semitism was still alive in Germany was fuelled at Christmas 1959 when two young neo-Nazis painted swastikas on the newly inaugurated synagogue in Cologne. During a visit to Israel by the Cologne Society for Christian-Jewish Cooperation that was taking place just at this time, the head of the Cologne education department contacted his counterpart in Tel Aviv. They agreed that to "confront young Germans with the reality of Israel" was the best antidote to anti-Semitism. Despite serious reservations in Tel Aviv, 35 youngsters from Cologne went to the city in 1960. Newspapers in Cologne took a close interest and questioned the young people on their return.

When the Federal Republic of Germany established diplomatic relations with Israel in 1966, stones were thrown at the German ambassador's car. However, German solidarity with Israel during the Six Day War in 1967 changed public opinion in Israel. The first visit to Cologne by teenagers from Tel Aviv was now possible. From 1968 onwards, an exchange programme was organised. School pupils from Cologne stayed with families in Tel Aviv, who sent their sons and daughters to Cologne in return. In 1979 an official twinning of the two cities was concluded. From difficult beginnings, partner programmes between schools in the two cities, cultural events and mutual visits are no longer exceptional today, but a normal occurrence.

Jewish Cemeteries

JEWISH CEMETERIES

Six Jewish cemeteries remain in Cologne. With the exception of the main cemetery that is still in use, they are not usually open to visitors, but tours take place on certain occasions and can be arranged on request.

BOCKLEMÜND

Part of the Westfriedhof, a large cemetery on the north-western edge of Cologne, is reserved for Jewish burials. As well as some 6,500 graves, there is a stone pyramid on the central axis commemorating Jewish soldiers who served in the First World War, a smaller memorial for 230 Cologne Jews who died in that conflict and a memorial to the victims of the Shoah (Holocaust), with a special plaque for Dr Isidor Caro, the last pre-war rabbi. The Lapidarium is an open loggia housing gravestones from the medieval cemetery dating from the 12th to the 15th century. The cemetery buildings were desi-gned by Robert Stern, architect of the synagogue in Ehrenfeld. The Hebrew inscription above the entrance is from the Book of Habakkuk: "The righteous will live by faith."

INFORMATION

Directions: Venloer Strasse, at the tram stop Bocklemünd (lines 3, 4). The cemetery is closed on Saturdays and Jewish holidays.
For detailed opening times, see www.sgk.de/gemeinde/friedhoefe

EHRENFELD

On the north-western side of Cologne's principal historic cemetery, Melaten, a small section for Jewish graves was laid out in 1899. The Ehrenfeld district had many Jewish residents, but from 1918 the cemetery in Bocklemünd became the preferred burial place for the community.

INFORMATION

◉ Entrance from Weinsbergstrasse
◷ 7am–8pm
🌐 melatenfriedhof.de

DECKSTEIN

The orthodox Adass Jeschurun congregation (→ p. 56), who noted and rejected the influence of Christian burial practices in other synagogue communities, established its own graveyard in west Cologne in 1910. No burials in coffins or urns were permitted, the gravestones are uniform and austere in style, and most bear inscriptions only in Hebrew letters. The cemetery was in use until the 1930s.

INFORMATION

◉ Decksteiner Straße
◷ not open to the public

MÜLHEIM

In the 375 years when they were banished from Cologne, Jews lived on the right bank of the Rhine in Mülheim, which was not incorporated into the city until 1914. The first Jews who moved to Cologne after the ban ended were Isaac and Sara Stern from Mülheim in 1798. A synagogue that existed before 1400 was destroyed in the ice flood of 1784, rebuilt, then devastated again in 1938 and demolished in 1956. Only a memorial plaque marks the site at Mülheimer Freiheit no. 78, but the cemetery, used from 1774 onwards, testifies to the former community. It was in use until 1942, and 100 graves remain.

INFORMATION

◉ Neurather Ring, immediately to the east of the rail tracks
◷ No regular opening hours

DEUTZ

Until the late 17th century, Jews from Deutz were buried across the Rhine in the ancient cemetery south of the city walls (see Judenbüchel). Following permission from the archbishop to establish a Jewish cemetery in Deutz, burials began in 1698 and continued until 1918, when the new cemetery in Bocklemünd opened. Many prominent persons found their last place of rest here, including Isaac Offenbach, cantor at the synagogue in Glockengasse and father of the composer Jacques Offenbach, Rahel Apfel (→ p. 76), and members of the Oppenheim banking family. The philosopher and early Zionist Moses Hess (→ p. 28) was buried here until 1961, when his remains were taken to Israel. The same had already happened to the graves of David Wolffsohn (→ p. 65) and his wife in 1952.

Between 1859 and 1882 the gravestones had to lie flat, as the Prussian military authorities required an unobstructed firing line here near their fortifications. Apart from the grand Oppenheim tomb, those in the northern section are mostly plain stones in the orthodox tradition inscribed with the names of the deceased. Later, as part of the Jewish community became more assimilated, the variety and ornamentation increased. The last burials took place in 1941. Today the cemetery is a valuable green space in a crowded city – more than 230 plant species have been identified there. The enclosure is not open to the public and has been desecrated in recent decades: in 1983, 63 graves were smashed during the Jewish festival of Sukkot, and in 1996 neo-Nazis daubed swastikas there.

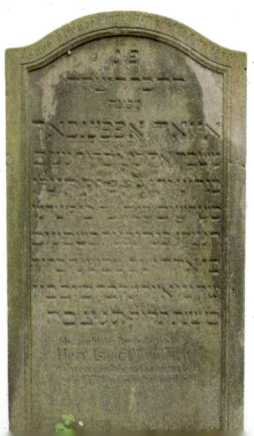

INFOS

◉ Judenkirchhofsweg

PORZ-ZÜNDORF

Freely accessible but forgotten and overgrown, the remains of a small cemetery for Jewish citizens of Zündorf, Wahn and Porz dating from

1923 can be found in woodland between the paths named Hasenkaul and Gartenweg. Eight graves, three of them without stones, have been identified.

➡ At the end of Tulpenweg, cross the tram lines and walk 300 metres east on Hasenkaul. A path on the left under trees leads to the graves. In the Porz district, the street named Carlebach-strasse was named after the last family of rabbis of the Adass Jeschurun ortho-dox community (→ p. 56).

JUDENBÜCHEL

The name Judenbüchel, meaning Jews' Hill, was given to a medieval burial ground to the south of the city wall. It was used by Jews until about 1696. The last traces of it were removed in 1936 to construct the wholesale market. The site is to the west of Bonner Strasse and north of Marktstrasse today. In the Middle Ages it was part of an open space that was used for tournaments and executions. The burial ground was in use in the 12th century, and the stone inscription in the cathedral dated 1266 states that Jews should be allowed to bury their dead there without disturbance.

The cemetery seems to have been damaged in the pogrom of 1349, as gravestones were reused as building material in the city hall. The cemetery remained in use by Jews from Deutz after the expulsion of the community from Cologne in 1424, but was later neglected and forgotten – except in the placename Judenbüchel – and was rediscovered during railway construc-tion in 1922. Some skeletons were reinterred in Bocklemünd at that time and in the 1930s, when the wholesale market was built. The Jewish tradition of a cemetery as a place of eternal rest was not respected.

A song in Cologne dialect by Willi Ostermann (1876–1936), who com-posed and wrote the texts of many Carnival hits, refers to the survival of the cemetery place name in popular memory: "It's peaceful and cosy at Am Dude Jüdd (The Dead Jew)" describes the scene in a place of entertainment of that name that was close to the site of the old Jewish burial ground.

TWO TERRIBLE MASSACRES

The pogrom of 1349 that eliminated the 800-strong Jewish community was not the first mass murder of Jews by Christians in Cologne.
In 1095 the pope had called on Christians to liberate Jerusalem
from the infidel and offered remission of sins for those who died as
crusaders. However, some preferred to kill non-Christians nearer to
home: in 1096, the year of the First Crusade, fanatical mobs passed
through the Rhineland, killing Jews and plundering their property.
Archbishop Hermann III of Cologne tried to protect "his" Jews by
dispersing them to smaller settlements outside the city, but most
were found there and massacred.

Miniature by Pierart dou Tielt illustrating the Tractatus quartus by Gilles li Muisit (Tournai, c. 1353). Title: "Gilles li Muisis, Antiquitates Flandriae (Tractatus quartus)".

The 14th century was marked by increasing anti-Semitism. When the Black Death killed about a third of the whole population of Europe in 1348-49, Jews were accused of poisoning wells. Pogroms took place along the river Rhine. The death of the archbishop, the supposed protector of the Jewish population, may have triggered events in Cologne. On the night of 23-24 August 1349, a mob stormed and burned the Jewish quarter. Few of its resi-dents survived. The layer of burned and smashed items found by archaeologists has shown the extent of the destruction. In 1953 a hoard of almost 300 gold and silver coins was discovered, buried in 1349 beneath a house that belonged to a Jew called Joel of Dortmund – a clear sign that Jewish citizens feared the future.

THE JEWISH COMMUNITY TODAY

From the first small gathering in the ruins of the synagogue in 1945, consisting of a handful of Jews who survived the war in hiding and few survivors from concentration camps, a Jewish community reformed and grew slowly in the 1950s. The decision to rebuild the synagogue on Roonstrasse/Rathenauplatz and its inauguration in 1959 showed that Jewish life had returned to Cologne on a permanent basis. By the 1980s, the community had approximately 1,300 members, but their high average age pointed to a difficult future.

A decisive change came with the collapse of the Communist bloc after 1989. The Federal Republic of Germany allowed immigration of Jews from the Soviet Union, and the Jewish population of Germany trebled within a decade. In 2010 the synagogue community in Cologne numbered approximately 5,000 persons, most of them from eastern Europe. Alongside the German-and-Hebrew prayer books in the synagogue lie the same texts in a German-and-Russian edition.

The ***Synagogengemeinde Köln*** (Cologne Synagogue Community) is a so-called "unified community" under German law, and benefits from a tax deducted by the state from members' salaries each month – in the

same way that income tax is deducted. This is the equivalent of the church tax that the German state collects from Roman Catholics and Protestants on behalf of their churches.

The unified community runs *educational and welfare institutions* in Ehrenfeld. This district of Cologne has strong Jewish associations from the past: a synagogue once stood there (only a memorial plaque remains, at Körnerstrasse no. 91) and the Israelitisches Asyl, a Jewish hospital and old persons' home that existed from 1908 until 1942. In the post-war years part of the war-damaged Asyl was used by Jewish institutions. The site was then occupied by a Belgian military hospital until the 1990s. Following renovation – a partial reconstruction and restoration of historic buildings, with new additions – it became the Jewish Welfare Centre in 2004, housing to a home for the elderly, a day centre for young children, a primary school, a synagogue and premises for social welfare of the community.

🌐 www.sgk.de/international/#english

Jews who prefer less orthodox religious practices formed a liberal congregation in 1996 (Gescher LaMassoret, → p.88) as an alternative to the unified community. *Gescher LaMassoret* has approximately 200 members and is registered as a society with charitable status, currently dependent on financial contributions from its members. The liberal Jewish community planned to convert a disused Christian chapel near Cologne's zoo into a synagogue. As the costs for alteration are too high for a small community, this project has been abandoned and temporary rooms are being used while Gescher LaMassoret look for permanent premises.

The name Gescher LaMassoret means "bridge to tradition", to emphasise the intention to live a contemporary life based on Jewish tradition. Here men and women are seated together to pray, whereas at the orthodox services in the synagogue on Roonstrasse the women sit separately in the gallery. The community website states that "we value gender equality in worship and in life" and that "Equality also means that the sexual orientation of our members does not matter to us as progressive Jews." For several years Gescher LaMassoret had a female rabbi.

JEWISH COMMUNITIES

Synagogen-Gemeinde Köln

The Jewish community in Cologne runs the synagogue in Roonstrasse (Rathenauplatz) and many other facilities: a home for elderly persons, a day-care centre for children, schools, prayer rooms, a mikveh and cemetery. Activities include the sports club Makkabi Köln and a women's group, as well as various social and educational services.

⊙ Ottostraße 85
© +49 (0)221 716220
⊕ www.sgk.de/international/#english

Gescher LaMassoret

The liberal Jewish community has met in recent years in various temporary venues.

© +49 (0)221 2870424
⊕ www.jlgk.de

MUSEUMS, MEMORIALS, CULTURE

MiQua – Museum in the Archaeological Quarter

The museum and archaeological trail on the Roman and Jewish history of Cologne is under construction and will not be completed until late 2027 at the earliest.
In the meantime, information is provided by a blog and events in the Rotes Haus, including talks and presentations of excavated items.

⊙ Rotes Haus, Alter Markt 21
⊕ miqua.blog/english

Kölnisches Stadtmuseum
City history museum (→ p. 40)
- ⊙ Minoritenstraße 11
- ⊘ Tue–Sun 10am–5pm, 1st Thursday
  of the month: 10am–10pm
- ⊕ www.koelnisches-stadtmuseum.de/en

NS-DOK
Memorial, exhibition and documentation centre for the victims of Nazi persecution, → p. 45
- ⊙ Appellhofplatz 23–25
- ⊘ Tue–Fri 10am–6pm, Sat–Sun 11am–6pm
- ⊕ museenkoeln.de/ns-dokumentationszentrum/Start-EN

Jawne – Yavne Memorial and Education Centre → p. 56
- ⊙ Erich-Klibansky-Platz 7,
  Access via Helenenstrasse
- ☎ 0175 2211620
- ⊘ Tue, Wed 11am–2pm, Thu 11am–2pm and
  4–7pm, Sun 12–4pm
- ⊕ www.jawne.de/en

Festival SHALOM-MUSIK.KOELN
A festival of Jewish music in Cologne and its region.
- ⊕ www.shalom-musik.koeln

OTHER INSTITUTIONS

Partnership association of Cologne and Tel Aviv-Yafo
Further information on German-language websites:
- ⊕ www.koelntelaviv.de/
- ⊕ www.facebook.com/koelntelaviv
- ⊕ www.stadt-koeln.de/artikel/70451/
  index.html

Germania Judaica
The extensive collection of written sources on Judaism in German is hosted by the Cologne city libraries. The central library is currently closed for renovation and has a temporary home at Hohe Strasse 68–82 (→ p.53).
- ⊕ germaniajudaica.de

Kölnische Gesellschaft für Christlich-Jüdische Zusammenarbeit e. V.
Since 1958 the Cologne Society for Christian-Jewish Cooperation has worked for dialogue between Christians and Jews and campaigned against persecution, anti-democratic tendencies and intolerance. It holds workshops, talks, readings and many other events.
- ⊙ Kartäusergasse 9–11
- ☎ +49 (0)221 3382225
- ⊕ www.koelnische-gesellschaft.de
  (website in German)

Deutsch-Israelische Gesellschaft

Cologne has an active branch of the German-Israeli Society, which runs events on cultural and political themes for the purpose of education about the state of Israel and the situation in the Middle East, and for combating anti-Semitism and anti-Zionism.

🌐 koeln.deutsch-israelische-gesellschaft.de

Kölsche Kippa Köpp

Cologne's Jewish Carnival society.

🌐 kippakoepp.koeln (in German only)

GUIDED TOURS

Synagogue

English-language tours of the synagogue in Roonstrasse/Rathenau-platz and the Jewish cemetery in Bocklemünd.

🌐 www.sgk.de/international/#english
📞 +49 /0)221 921560-82
✉ e.bugaeva@sgk.de

Rhenania Judaica

A group of professional city guides runs tours in Cologne and the Rhineland in English and German on Jewish themes, e.g. Jewish history in the Old Town, the origins of Zionism, Jewish participation in Carnival, Jewish life in the 19th and early 20th century, persecution under the Nazis.

🌐 rhenaniajudaica.de

Cologne Cathedral

Depictions of Jews in the cathedral and the relations between Jews and Christians in the Middle Ages and later are the theme of special cathedral tours in English and German.
Bookings through:

📍 Domforum, Domkloster 3
📞 +49 (0)221 92584730
🌐 www.domforum.de

THEMED GIFTS

The online shop of Judaica Cologne presents a range of products bearing motifs from Jewish Cologne – from postcards, greetings cards and notebooks to coffee mugs, tote bags, hoodies and more.

🌐 judaicacologne.de

KOSHER AND ISRAELI RESTAURANTS

Although there is no local kosher butcher, the restaurant *Mazal Tov* in the synagogue in Roonstrasse prepares strictly supervised kosher dishes for private celebrations– weddings, family celebrations, bar and bat mitzvahs, meals for guests of the synagogue and other occasions on request.

Two restaurants in Cologne serve delicious, non-kosher Israeli food:

Nish Nush

"Nish nush" is the Hebrew word for a snack. Here you can enjoy excellent, filling Israeli street food, including typical Middle Eastern dishes such as shakshuka, hummus, falafel and filled pita bread. There is a wide choice for vegans and vegetarians.

⊙ Aachener Straße 14
© +49 (0)221 42335009
⊕ nish-nush.de

Getränkemarkt Beethoven – Koscherland

Sale of Israeli products and kosher food.

⊙ Beethovenstrasse 33, 50674 Köln
  (a short distance from the synagogue in Roonstrasse)
© +49 (0)221 801730
⊕ www.koscherland.de

NENI

In a relaxed atmosphere on the 8th floor of the hip 25hours Hotel with a superb all-round view of Cologne's city centre from the terrace and the adjoining Monkey Bar, excellent food and wines from Israel are served. NENI stands for Nuriel, Elior, Nadiv and Ilan, the four sons of the Molcho family, who have brought their culinary success story to more than ten European cities.

Leave room for desserts: a choice of three different sweets served on a tiered tray rounds off the meal in style.

⊙ Im Klapperhof 22
© +49 (0)221 16253561
⊕ nenifood.com/restaurants/koln

70 CE	Destruction of the Second Temple in Jerusalem by the Romans, generally considered as the start of the diaspora, the scattering of Jews across many countries, although Jewish communities already existed in regions around the Mediterranean.
321	First written evidence of Jewish settlement: a letter written by the court of Emperor Constantine to the city council in Cologne allows the admission of Jews
800	A Jew named Isaac takes part in a delegation to the caliph of Baghdad on behalf of Emperor Charlemagne and returns in 802; he is the first Jew known by name who is active in the Rhineland.
11th century	Early in the century, a synagogue is built close to the present city hall of Cologne.
1075	Cologne Jews mourn the death of Archbishop Anno, their protector, in the synagogue.
1096	During the First Crusade, a mob destroys the synagogue. Jews take refuge in the houses of Christian citizens and are later dispersed by the archbishop to outlying villages, where many are later found and killed or commit suicide.
1106	The city wall is extended. The Jewish community has the duty to defend the "Jews' Gate" (no longer existent; it stood at the south end of the street Kattenbug).
c. 1250	Ascher ben Jechiel, author of major religious and literary works, is born in the Rhineland and spends part of his life in Cologne.

1266	Archbishop Engelbert II's stone inscription in Cologne Cathedral confirms the rights of the Jews.
c. 1280	A new bimah for the reading of the Torah is made, almost certainly by masons of the cathedral workshop, with a cellar beneath it.
c. 1300	The Jewish quarter expands in this period, according to records of land ownership.
1349	During the Black Death, a mob burns and storms the Jewish quarter in Cologne, causing great destruction and killing most of the Jewish population.
1372	A small number of Jews move to Cologne, but the community does not regain its former prosperity.
1404	The city council of Cologne specifies details of the clothing that Jews must wear in the city.
1424	The city council of Cologne expels all Jews from the city "for all eternity".
1426	The synagogue is converted to a chapel for the city hall.
1695	The Jewish community in Deutz – at that time not part of the city of Cologne – establishes a cemetery.
1798	Under French rule, Jews are allowed to live in Cologne for the first time since 1424.
1801	18 families formally establish a Jewish community; by 1808, 170 Jews are living in Cologne.
1861	Opening of the new synagogue in Glockengasse, designed by the cathedral architect Zwirner and paid for by the banker Abraham Oppenheim.

1869	Jewish citizens of the North German Confederation of states are given full civil rights; two years later this applies in the whole of the newly founded German Empire.
1884	The synagogue of the Orthodox Adass Jeschurun community is built in St.-Apern-Strasse.
1896	Max Bodenheimer publishes the Cologne Theses – principles for founding a Jewish state in Palestine that were adopted by the Zionist movement.
1899	A new synagogue for the liberal Jewish community in Roonstrasse is completed.
1914	Start of the First World War, in which 22,000 Jewish soldiers died on the German side.
1925	The Jewish population of Cologne is approx. 25,000.
1933	Boycott of Jewish businesses on April 1 by the National Socialists.
1935	The Nuremberg Laws deprive Jewish citizens of civil rights and prohibit mixed marriages.
1938	Synagogues and other Jewish institutions are attacked and burned in the pogrom night on 9–10 November.
1939	Dr Erich Klibansky, director of the Jawne Jewish school, organises the emigration of some 130 children to England.

1941	In May the Gestapo orders the removal of Jews from their homes to "ghetto houses", from where they are deported to death camps and ghettoes in eastern Europe from October onwards.
1945	Approximately 40 Jews who survived the war in hiding remain in Cologne.
1959	The synagogue in Roonstrasse is reopened.
1960	The first visit to Tel Aviv by school pupils from Cologne.
1979	Representatives of the cities of Tel Aviv and Cologne sign a twinning agreement.
1997	The Lion Fountain, commemorating 1,100 Jewish children murdered during the Nazi years, is unveiled on Erich-Klibansky-Platz next to the Yavne Memorial Centre.
2003/4	Jewish welfare institutions including a home for senior citizens, a kindergarten and a primary school move to premises in Ottostrasse in the Ehrenfeld district.
2021	Events are held to mark the 1,700th anniversary of the first surviving written record of Jewish settlement in Cologne.

AUTHOR

John Sykes was born in Southport near Liverpool and has lived for over 40 years in Cologne, where his main themes as a city guide are Cologne Cathedral and Jewish history. He is the author of travel guides for German visitors to England and writes about his long-distance walk around the English coast on www.beatingthebounds.eu.